Analogue Guide

London

Contents

London

—Welcome to Analogue London

London has played a significant role in world affairs to a greater or lesser extent since it was founded as a Roman settlement in the year 50, a long time ago even by English standards. As capital of the British Empire on which the sun famously never set, Victorian London was chosen as the baseline for international time conventions, making it quite literally the centre of the world. Subsequent decades of relative decline eventually gave way to the rise of "Cool Britannia" in the 1990s, and the opening of its borders to talent from across the globe.

Today, London is arguably the most international global city, and one in three Londoners was born abroad. Many feared the end of the good life when the money-spinning City stumbled in 2008, but the crisis had little impact on London's attraction to newcomers. Aside from its traditional connections to the Commonwealth, and its more recent favour among the worldwide oligarchy, London has also turned into somewhat of a *euro*-melting pot—quite a feat in a country that for centuries has defined itself against the madness of affairs on the Continent.

No Londoner worth his salt would ever admit to anything more than merely "quite liking it", but it would be hard to imagine a city as multifaceted not offering something new and inspiring for everyone—from the convivial pubs of Clerkenwell and the recent influx of Iberian and Antipodean influences on the culinary scene, to the cutting edge art and design of the East End and the ideal of postcard pretty Notting Hill.

We've aspired to unearth the best of all of this, with photographs and maps throughout. Enjoy!

Neighbourhoods

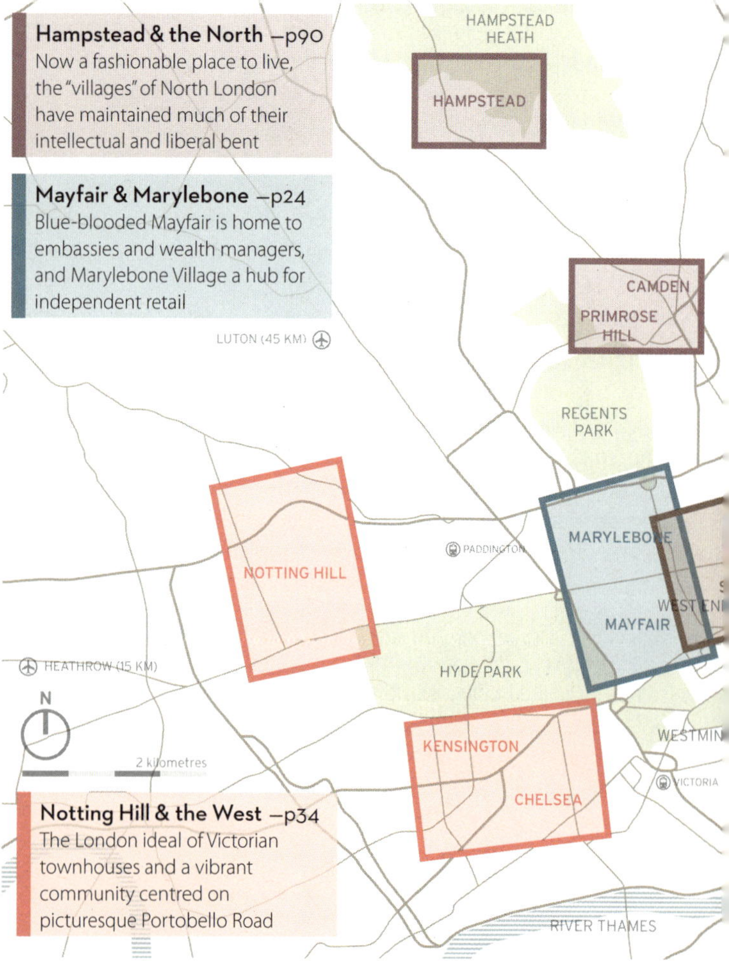

Hampstead & the North —p90
Now a fashionable place to live, the "villages" of North London have maintained much of their intellectual and liberal bent

Mayfair & Marylebone —p24
Blue-blooded Mayfair is home to embassies and wealth managers, and Marylebone Village a hub for independent retail

LUTON (45 KM) ✈

HAMPSTEAD
HEATH

HAMPSTEAD

CAMDEN

PRIMROSE
HILL

REGENTS
PARK

MARYLEBONE

🚉 PADDINGTON

NOTTING HILL

WEST END

MAYFAIR

✈ HEATHROW (15 KM)

HYDE PARK

WESTMIN

N

2 kilometres

KENSINGTON

🚉 VICTORIA

CHELSEA

Notting Hill & the West —p34
The London ideal of Victorian townhouses and a vibrant community centred on picturesque Portobello Road

RIVER THAMES

Soho & Covent Garden —p8

London's urban core is packed with restaurants, bars, retail and entertainment, and what remains of its less salubrious past

Clerkenwell & Islington —p62

A former light manufacturing hub and left-wing print shop, the area's lofts and terraces are now home to media and advertising types

Shoreditch & the East —p48

The East End has morphed into an interesting hotchpotch of its down heeled past and its reincarnation as the city's new artistic epicentre

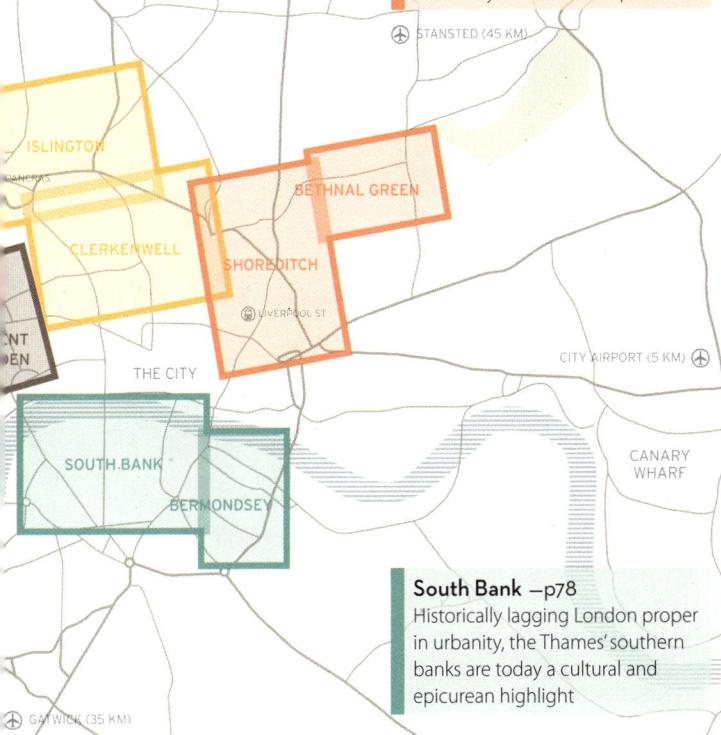

STANSTED (45 KM)

ISLINGTON

PANCRAS

BETHNAL GREEN

CLERKENWELL

SHOREDITCH

LIVERPOOL ST

NT
EN

THE CITY

CITY AIRPORT (5 KM)

SOUTH.BANK

CANARY
WHARF

BERMONDSEY

South Bank —p78

Historically lagging London proper in urbanity, the Thames' southern banks are today a cultural and epicurean highlight

GATWICK (35 KM)

Soho & Covent Garden

—24-Hour Urban Core

Soho has long held a reputation as the focal point of London's nightlife—from the theatres of the West End to the nightclubs off Old Compton and Dean Streets, to what remains of the area's heritage as a seedy red light district. Densely packed with restaurants, bars and coffee shops, Soho is the closest that London comes to a 24-hour city. The area is also a centre of creative and media businesses, notably from the film industry.

Despite early efforts to develop Soho along the lines of grander Mayfair and Bloomsbury, the area never caught on with the wealthy; those who could had moved out by the mid-18th century. Subsequent decades of immigration and neglect turned its streets into a hotbed of prostitution and artistry, shaping the quirky identity that Soho enjoys today. South of Shaftsbury Avenue, pedestrianized Gerrard Street is the heart of London's Chinatown. To the north, beneath the 1960s-glamour BT Tower, Fitzrovia is home to advertising agencies and architectural firms, along with an increasingly interesting array of culinary offerings.

Covent Garden, Soho's less brash sibling across the Charing Cross Road, has seen its fortunes tied to its fruit and vegetable market. The neoclassical market hall, erected in 1830, had outgrown its purposes by the 1960s, and the market was moved out. The neighbourhood became popular with new residents in the 1980s when the market hall re-opened as a shopping centre. Today, Covent Garden is a popular retail destination, with pockets of sophistication around Neil's Yard and the Seven Dials. To its north, the literary and academic enclave of Bloomsbury is the birthplace of literary modernism and home to the British Museum.

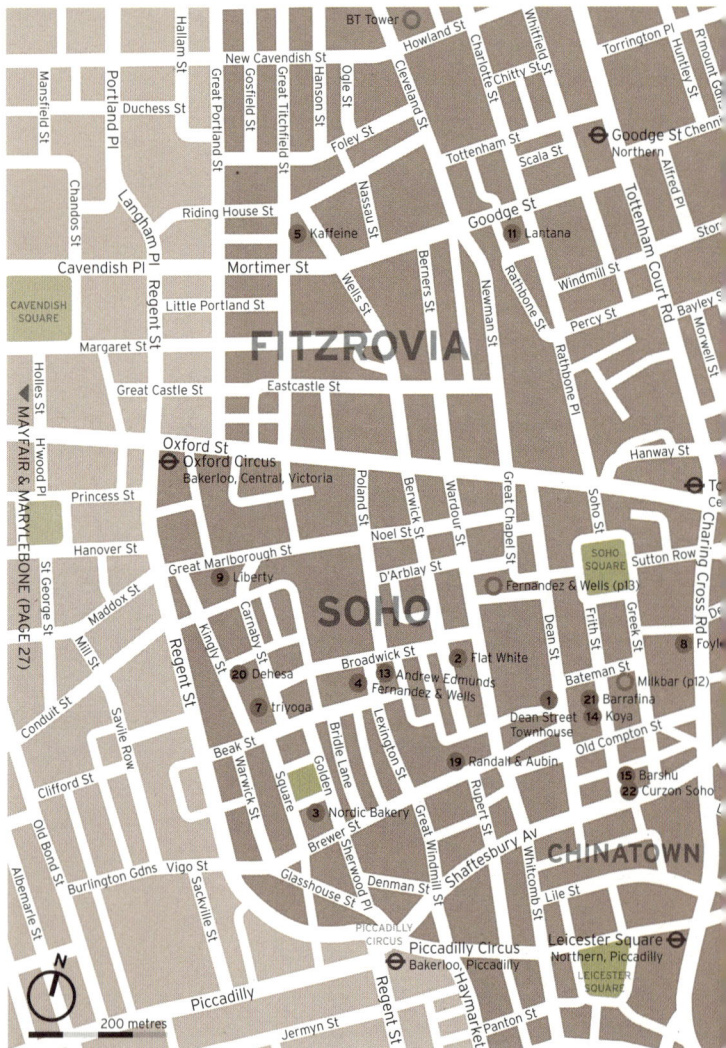

BT Tower

Hallam St
New Cavendish St
Howland St
Whitfield St
Torrington Pl
Rimount Gdns
Huntley St

Portland Pl
Gosfield St
Great Titchfield St
Hanson St
Ogle St
Chitty St
Cleveland St
Charlotte St

Mansfield St
Duchess St
Foley St
Tottenham St
Alfred St

Chandos St
Langham Pl
Riding House St
Nassau St
Goodge St
Scala St
Goodge St Chenni
Northern

Cavendish Pl
5 Kaffeine
Berners St
Newman St
Rathbone St
Windmill St
Percy St
11 Lantana

Little Portland St
Mortimer St
Wells St
Rathbone Pl
Bayley St
Morwell S

CAVENDISH
SQUARE
Margaret St
Regent St

FITZROVIA

Great Castle St
Eastcastle St

Holles St
Hwood Pl
MAYFAIR & MARYLEBONE (PAGE 27)
Oxford St
Oxford Circus
Bakerloo, Central, Victoria
Hanway St

Princess St
Poland St
Berwick St
Wardour St
Great Chapel St
Soho St
To
Ce
Charing Cross Rd

Hanover St
Noel St
SOHO
SQUARE
Sutton Row
Fernandez & Wells (p13)

St George St
Maddox St
Great Marlborough St
9 Liberty
D'Arblay St
SOHO
Dean St
Frith St
Greek St
8 Foyle

Mill St
Kingly St
Carnaby St
Broadwick St
2 Flat White
Bateman St
Milkbar (p12)

20 Dehesa
13 Andrew Edmunds
Fernandez & Wells
Lexington St
21 Barratina
14 Koya

Conduit St
Savile Row
7 itrivoga
4
1
Dean Street
Townhouse
Old Compton St

Clifford St
Beak St
Warwick St
Bridle Lane
Golden
19 Randall & Aubin
Rupert St
15 Barshu
22 Curzon Soho

Old Bond St
Burlington Gdns
Vigo St
Brewer St
3 Nordic Bakery
Sherwood
Great Windmill St
Shaftesbury Av
Whitcomb St
CHINATOWN

Albemarle St
Sackville St
Glasshouse St
Denman St
Windmill
Lile St

Regent St
PICCADILLY
CIRCUS
Piccadilly Circus
Bakerloo, Piccadilly
Leicester Square
Northern, Piccadilly
LEICESTER
SQUARE

Piccadilly
Jermyn St
Haymarket
Panton St

200 metres

PAGE 10   SOHO & COVENT GARDEN

Torrington Sq

Bedford Way

Renoir Cinema (p22)

Bernard St

CORAM'S FIELDS

Russell Square
Piccadilly

Guilford St

Lamb's Conduit St

Milman St

John St

RUSSELL SQUARE

Russell Sq

Bedford Pl

Southampton Row

Great Ormond St

Orde Hall St

18 Cigala
Rugby St

Montague Pl

Montague St

Old Gloucester St

Boswell St

Great James St

Northington St

Harpur St

Jockey's Fields

BLOOMSBURY

British Museum

BLOOMSBURY SQUARE

Theobald's Rd

Drake St

Princeton St

Red Lion St

Brownlow St

▶ CLERKENWELL (PAGE 64)

Bloomsbury St

Coptic St

Museum St

Bury Pl

Bloomsbury Way

Southampton Row

Catton St

Eagle St

Rd

New Oxford St

Holborn
Central, Piccadilly

16 Shanghai Blues

High Holborn

High St

High Holborn

Newton St

Kingsway

Endell St

Drury Lane

Stukeley St

Shorts Gardens

Mackin St

Remnant St

Newman's Row

Shelton St

Betterton St

Parker St

Great Queen St

17 Great Queen Street

LINCOLN'S INN FIELDS

e 6

triyoga (p15)

Arne St

Wild St

Keeley St

Sardinia St

New Sq

Serle St

12 Canela

Shelton St

Neal St

Bow St

COVENT GARDEN

Portugal St

Carey St

Mercer St

Covent Garden
Piccadilly

Floral St

Russell St

Catherine St

Aldwych

King St

Covent Garden Market

Bedford St

Henrietta St

Tavistock St

Exeter St

10 Somerset House

Strand

Fleet St

Maiden Lane

▼ SOUTHBANK (PAGE 80)

Edwardian Soho Revived
Dean St Townhouse

① 69-71 Dean St, at Meard St
+44 20 7434 1775
deanstreettownhouse.com
⊖⊖ Tottenham Court Road,
⊖⊖ Piccadilly Circus
Doubles from £260 incl. tax (Tiny
rooms from £220 incl. tax); excl.
breakfast, available in-house.

Dean Street Townhouse offers
a slice of history in the thick of
Soho without eschewing any
of the warmth and luxury of a
contemporary boutique hotel.
Housed in the former Gargoyle
Club, the haunt of artists the likes
of Francis Bacon and Lucien Freud,
the space was converted into a
thirty-nine bedroom hotel in 2009.
Located at the corner of gorgeous
cobble-stoned Meard Street,
the Townhouse is but a stone's
throw from many of London's
best restaurants, museums and
entertainment.

Antipodean Coffee Highlight
Flat White

② 17 Berwick St, between Broadwick
St and Peter St
+44 20 7734 0370
flatwhitecafe.com
⊖⊖ Piccadilly Circus,
⊖⊖⊖ Oxford Circus
Open daily. Mon-Fri 8am-7pm; Sat/
Sun 9am-6pm.

Flat White does antipodean coffee
and brunch-on-the-go at its
absolute best. The flat whites at
this establishment are so smooth
that even the most discerning
connoisseur will gasp with delight
at the first sip. Grab a table amidst
the local media types, delve
into a copy of one of the design
magazines on offer and indulge in a
toasted banana bread slice or some
scrambled eggs. Flat White's sister
establishment Milkbar, located a
few blocks away, is equally enticing.

Nordic Café

Nordic Bakery

🌑 14a Golden Sq, between Lower
James St and Lower John St
+44 20 3230 1077
nordicbakery.com
🚇🚇 Piccadilly Circus
Open daily. Mon-Fri 8am-8pm; Sat
9am-7pm; Sun 11am-7pm.

One of the most serene spots in
central London, Nordic Bakery
is a haven for fresh baked
Nordic delicacies, such as warm
kanelbulle and *smörgås* open-faced
sandwiches, served up alongside
excellent espresso based drinks.
The Golden Square location is
bang in the middle of Soho and
patrons include media types
stopping in for a break from the
surrounding creative offices. Floor
to ceiling windows allow for unique
views of Soho life and the interior
design is dotted with elements by
Alvar Aalto, Kaj Franck and Ilmari
Tapiovaara.

Coffee & Charcuterie

Fernandez & Wells

🌑 43 Lexington St, between Beak St
and Broadwick St
+44 20 7734 1546
fernandezandwells.com
🚇🚇🚇 Oxford Circus,
🚇🚇 Piccadilly Circus
Open daily. Mon-Fri 11am-10pm; Sat/
Sun noon-10pm. Beak St café: Mon-
Fri 7.30am-6pm; Sat 9am-6pm; Sun
9am-5pm.

Fernandez & Wells' fabulous quartet
of locations specialize in the best
of British and continental produce
in a resolutely English setting.
Nestled on quaint Lexington Street,
this branch features a sumptuous
spread of delights—so whether
it's a thirty-six month cured *jamón
ibérico de bellota* sandwich drizzled
with olive oil or a sip of premium
sherry you're after, you will find
it in its absolute finest form at
Fernandez & Wells.

Caffeinated Fitzrovia

Kaffeine

⑤ 66 Great Titchfield St, at Little
Titchfield St
+44 20 7580 6755
kaffeine.co.uk
⊖⊖⊖ Oxford Circus, ⊖ Goodge
Street
Open daily. Mon-Fri 7.30am-6pm; Sat
9am-6pm; Sun 9.30am-5pm.

Kaffeine is another prime example
of antipodean influence on the
London coffee scene, taking
specialities such as the flat white
and long black to dizzying new
levels of perfection with the help
of a stellar Synesso Cyncra espresso
machine. Patrons will delight in
Kaffeine's simultaneously carefree
and relaxing ambiance. An brick-
backed bar leads to cosy wood-
panelled seating at the rear of the
long but intimate space.

Coffee Pioneer

Monmouth Coffee

⑥ 27 Monmouth St, between Seven
Dials and Shaftsbury Av
+44 20 7232 3010
monmouthcoffee.co.uk
⊖ Covent Garden, ⊖⊖ Tottenham
Court Road
Closed Sun. Mon-Sat 8am-6.30pm.

Roasting and retailing beans since
1978, Monmouth's original café
location in the heart of Covent
Garden's Seven Dials area serves
decadently strong single cone filter
coffee, espresso based drinks and
a staggering array of pastries in a
warm and convivial setting. The
tiny space is decked out with rough
slabs of wood and the aroma of
freshly ground coffee percolates
every corner. Monmouth's Borough
Market (p83) location allows
patrons to soak up the bucolic
atmosphere of the surrounding
market stalls.

Yoga Studio

triyoga

7 Kingly Court, 2nd Floor, between
Kingly St and Carnaby St
+44 20 7483 3344
triyoga.co.uk
⊖⊖⊖ Oxford Circus,
⊖⊖ Piccadilly Circus
Classes daily. Drop-ins from £13.
Mats available free of charge.

Triyoga offers a vast range of
high quality yoga, pilates and
gyrotonics classes, as well as scores
of treatments to complement
one's practice. Atypical for its
central London location, the Soho
branch offers ample studio space,
complete with charming views of
the panoply of surrounding central
London rooftops. The Primrose Hill
location (map p93) also boasts a
relaxing café.

Independent Bookshop

Foyles

8 113-119 Charing Cross Rd, between
Manette St and Old Compton St
+44 20 7437 5660
foyles.co.uk
⊖⊖ Tottenham Court Road
Open daily. Mon-Sat 9.30am-9pm;
Sun 11.30am-6pm.

Established in 1903, book trader
Foyles' flagship location offers five
floors replete with a cornucopia
of two hundred thousand books,
covering every topic imaginable.
The shop also boasts a superior
selection of music, a jazz café
overlooking bustling Charing Cross
Road, and an in-house outlet of
Grant and Cutler, the UK's most
extensive purveyor of foreign
language books. Readings and
events are regularly scheduled.

Fashion & Design Temple

Liberty

● Great Marlborough St, between Kingly St and Carnaby St
+44 20 7734 1234
liberty.co.uk
⊖⊖⊖ Oxford Circus
Open daily. Mon-Sat 10am-8pm; Sun noon-6pm.

Arthur Liberty's design emporium has been at the forefront of home wares and fashion since its inception in 1875. The store's colourful history is reflected in the magnificent Art Nouveau designs it pioneered in the 1920s. The founder's vision propelled him to travel the globe to source exquisite artefacts and fabrics to put on display in his ever-expanding central London outlet. Today, Liberty's famously mock tudor shop remains at the vanguard of fashion and design and is a highlight of the London shopping circuit.

Visual Arts Hub

Somerset House

● Strand, at Lancaster Pl
+44 20 7845 4600
somersethouse.org.uk
⊖⊖ Temple, ⊖ Covent Garden
Open daily. Galleries and Embankment Level: 10am-6pm; River Terrace 8am-11pm.

Addressing London's lack of grand public buildings, the neoclassical Somerset House was envisioned in the late 18th century as a home for the learned societies (see RA, p29) and various public offices. Soon dominated by the Empire's growing bureaucracy, the complex was gradually reallocated to the arts over the past few decades. Today, its galleries show contemporary art and design exhibitions, and its office space is made available to the creative industries. The fountain courtyard hosts open-air concerts and film screenings in the summer, and an ice rink in the winter.

Antipodean Fitzrovia

Lantana

⓫ 13-14 Charlotte Pl, between Goodge St and Rathbone St
+44 20 7637 3347
lantanacafe.co.uk
⊖ Goodge St, ⊖⊖ Tottenham Court Road
Open daily. Mon-Fri 8am-6pm; Sat/Sun 9am-5pm.

A convivial Australian owned café in central Fitzrovia, Lantana specializes in breakfast and brunch. This is also a relaxing spot to kick back with an espresso or a glass of wine in the late afternoon. During the summer months, open windows and outdoor seating give way to cosmopolitan Charlotte Place, a picturesque alley in the midst of Fitzrovia's creative agencies and architectural practices.

Portuguese/Brazilian Café

Canela

⓬ 33 Earlham St, between Seven Dials and Neal St
+44 20 7240 6926
canelacafe.com
⊖ Covent Garden, ⊖⊖ Tottenham Court Road
Open daily. Mon-Wed 9.30am-10.30pm; Thu/Fri 9.30am-11.30pm; Sat 10.30am-11.30pm; Sun 10.30am-8pm.

If you fancy a hearty *feijoada* stew with a glass of velvety alentejano wine followed by a *cafezinho* with its own cinnamon stick in a warm contemporary Portuguese setting, Canela is the place to go. An appealing mid-shopping coffee and homemade cake stop, the café/restaurant is also a delightful setting for a full meal in a relaxed and affable ambiance with a distinctly urban backdrop.

Cosy Soho Dining

Andrew Edmunds

13 46 Lexington St, between
Broadwick St and Beak St
+44 20 7437 5708
⊖⊖⊖ Oxford Circus,
⊖⊖ Piccadilly Circus
Open daily. Lunch Mon-Fri 12.30pm-
3pm; Sat/Sun 1pm-3.15pm. Dinner
Mon-Sat 6pm-10.30pm; Sun 6pm-
10.15pm.

This charmingly rough and tumble
restaurant on quaint Lexington
street offers classic Continental
home cooking and an alluringly
unique wine list with French
tendencies. Small tables and a
whimsically uneven wooden floor
add to the restaurant's appeal.
Andrew Edmunds is an excellent
spot for a romantic *tête-à-tête* in a
warm but unfussy atmosphere.

Udon Specialist

Koya

14 49 Frith St, between Bateman St
and Old Compton St
+44 20 7434 4463
koya.co.uk
⊖⊖ Tottenham Court Road
Open daily. Lunch Mon-Sun noon-
3pm. Dinner Mon-Sat 5.30pm-
10.30pm; Sun 5.30pm-10pm.

Koya offers the chance to indulge
in a top-notch bowl of homemade
Udon noodles in an unruffled and
welcoming setting. The simple,
bright dining room merges wood
with tile, and the bar area at the
rear allows for a behind-the-scenes
glimpse into the creation process of
Udon. Dishes range from Atsu-Atsu
(hot noodle with hot broth) to Hiya-
Hiya (cold noodle with cold sauce)
and the combined cold-hot delight
known as Hiya-Atsu—all in several
different incarnations.

Sichuanese Spice

Barshu

15 28 Frith St, at Romilly St
+44 20 7287 8822
bar-shu.co.uk
⊖⊖ Leicester Square
Mon-Thu/Sun noon-11pm; Fri/Sat
noon-11.30pm.

A fabulously spicy Sichuanese
restaurant in the midst of bustling
Soho, Barshu cooks up the ultimate
remedy for a lengthy bout of
London fog. Ornate wooden
carvings decorate both levels of
the restaurant, and buzzing Frith
Street is always within eyeshot. The
menu includes a generous range
of excellent and authentically fiery
dishes. Located on the same block
as the Curzon Soho cinema (p22),
Barshu makes for excellent pre or
post-movie dining.

Shanghai Style & Cuisine

Shanghai Blues

16 193-197 High Holborn, at New
Oxford St
+44 20 7404 1668
shanghaiblues.co.uk
⊖⊖ Holborn
Open daily noon-5pm, 5.30pm-late.

Housed in an elegant listed
building and former library on
High Holborn, Shanghai Blues
concocts a range of Shanghainese
delights to be enjoyed in one of
the space's elegantly clad multilevel
dining rooms, mezzanine lounge
or bar. Just around the corner from
both Soho and Covent Garden,
the restaurant offers an elegant
space within short proximity of the
buzz. Its location at the nexus of
Covent Garden and Bloomsbury
contributes to a highly diverse
clientele of bankers, expats, locals,
media types, journalists and
academics.

Great British Cuisine

Great Queen Street

17 32 Great Queen St, between Drury Lane and Kingsway
+44 20 7242 0622
🚇 Holborn
Open daily. Lunch Mon-Sat noon-2.30pm; Sun 1pm-4pm. Dinner Mon-Sat 6pm-10.30pm.

This charmingly discrete and dimly lit restaurant at the fringes of Covent Garden offers outstanding fresh seasonal fare, artfully whipped into modern British classics. Great Queen Street's sophisticated menu, wine list and clientele add luster and flair to a neighbourhood generally associated with retail therapy. The imposing art deco Freemason's Hall across the street is a sight to behold.

Spanish Bloomsbury

Cigala

18 54 Lamb's Conduit St, at Rugby St
+44 20 7405 1717
cigala.co.uk
🚇 Russell Square, 🚇 Holborn
Open daily. Mon-Fri noon-10.45pm; Sat 12.30pm-10.45pm; Sun 12.30pm-9.45pm.

An authentic Spanish restaurant on thriving Lamb's Conduit Street, Cigala is at once low-key and uncompromisingly quality driven. Chef and owner Jake Hodges, a co-founder of Moro (p75), sources many of the ingredients directly from Spain. The restaurant's uneven stone and floor-to-ceiling windowed exterior give way to a decidedly Continental interior, decorated with clean lines, crisp white table cloths and warm wood panelling. The outside terrace is a delightful place to enjoy a meal in warmer months.

Oysters & Champagne

Randall & Aubin

19 16 Brewer St, between Lexington St and Wardour St
+44 20 7287 4447
randallandaubin.com
⊖⊖ Piccadilly Circus
Open daily. Mon-Wed noon-11pm; Thu-Sat noon-midnight; Sun noon-10pm.

Randall & Aubin is a celebratory space, drawing in Soho's crackling energy, while revelling in its own discrete panache. The ultimate spot to crack open a bottle of champagne to marry with oysters or any of the other seafood and charcuterie on offer. The site of the restaurant was originally a butcher specialising in the best of Paris and British produce. Inspired by these roots, Randall & Aubin's menu reflects the space's heritage with stellar results.

Jamón Specialist

Dehesa

20 25 Ganton St, at Kingly St
+44 20 7494 4170
dehesa.co.uk
⊖⊖⊖ Oxford Circus
Open daily. Mon-Fri noon-3pm, 5pm-11pm; Sat noon-11pm; Sun noon-5pm.

Named after the acclaimed Spanish site where the prized acorn fed *jamón ibérico de bellota* is found, Dehesa is a sophisticated Spanish and Italian inspired charcuterie and wine bar tucked away from the nearby shopping frenzy of Regent and Carnaby Streets. Bathed in warm light to complement the coffee colored seating and luxurious wooden tables, the interior exudes an air of comfort and class. In warmer months, the outdoor patio allows patrons some face time with the frenetically charged media types and shoppers whirling around Soho.

Convivial Tapas Bar
Barrafina

21 54 Frith St, between Bateman St and Old Compton St
barrafina.co.uk
⊖⊖ Tottenham Court Road
Open daily. Lunch Mon-Sat noon-3pm; Sun 1pm-3.30pm. Dinner Mon-Sat 5pm-11pm; Sun 5.30pm-10pm.

Located in the throbbing core of Frith Street, Barrafina soaks in all the local pizazz while retaining a uniquely nonchalant but perennially fashionable flair. Tapas are incredibly fresh and artfully prepared and the wine list is excellent. So take a seat at the marble bar, indulge in that *jamón de jabugo* with a scintillating glass of Verdejo from Rueda and mingle with the crowd.

Independent Film and Drinks
Curzon Soho

22 99 Shaftesbury Av, between Frith St and Greek St
+44 330 500 1331
curzoncinemas.com
⊖⊖ Leicester Square
Screenings daily. Refer to website for showtimes. Tickets £12.50

The Curzon group's five cinemas, scattered throughout London, screen the best of contemporary film. The Curzon Soho also boasts a lively street-side Konditor & Cook café, serving delightful pastries alongside frothy cappuccinos. The popular full bar downstairs makes an experience at this bastion of international independent and arthouse cinema refreshingly unique.

Mayfair & Marylebone
—Blue Blooded and Quintessentially English

Grand yet understated, Mayfair is the quintessentially English centre of aristocratic London life. Less residential that it once was, its magnificent Edwardian and Georgian real estate now houses embassies, wealth managers and hedge funds, as well as some of London's most exclusive boutiques. Marylebone, no less aristocratic in its heritage, but arguably more democratic in feel, has become an interesting destination for independent retail.

Well-heeled from the outset and situated just adjacent to the expanses of Hyde Park, Mayfair was originally developed as a fashionable residential district. To this day, the Duke of Westminster and the Grosvenor family own much of the underlying freehold land. As many of the neighbourhood's wealthy residents gravitated towards the leafy streets of Kensington, the area became the preferred corporate headquarters of Britain plc. Today, Mayfair is renowned for its high-end fashion and art scene, notably around Bond and Dover Streets, as well as the bespoke tailoring of Savile Row. The offerings of Mayfair itself stand in stark contrast to the predictable retail mix of Oxford Street and more elegant Regent Street, its boundaries to the north and east respectively.

Marylebone was commissioned by its landlords in the 18th century as a residential neighbourhood on a rational street grid. The neighbourhood long lived in the shadow of grander Mayfair. However, more recently the streets around Marylebone High Street, also known as Marylebone Village, have turned into an attractive hub for independent shops—not to an insignificant degree due to careful lease management by its landowner, the Howard de Walden Estate.

Map labels

▲ FITZROVIA (PAGE 10)

Albany St
Park Sq East
REGENT'S PARK
Regent's Park
Park Sq West
Outer Circle
York Terrace East
York Terrace West
Allsop Pl
Harley St
Devonshire Place
Nottingham Pl
Luxborough St
Chiltern St
Baker St
Bickenhall St
Gloucester Place
Marylebone Rd
Melcombe St
Balcome St
Upper Montague St
Knox St
Wyndham St
Enford St

Great Portland St
Bolsover St
Great Portland St
Hallam St
Park Crescent
Portland Pl
Carburton St
Clipstone St
New Cavendish St
Duchess St
Portland Pl
Mansfield St
Chandos St
Gosfield St
Langham St
Riding House St
Mortimer St
Little Portland St
Langham Pl
Cavendish Pl
Regent St
Margaret St
CAVENDISH SQUARE

Bakerloo
Metropolitan
Baker Loo

Upper Wimpole St
Devonshire St
Beaumont St
Weymouth St
Marylebone St
Marylebone High St
Paddington St
Manchester St
Dorset St
Rodmarton St
Blandford St
Montague Pl
Crawford St
Montagu Pl
Montague Sq
Byanston Sq
Wyndham Pl

Nordic Bakery (p13)
Wimpole St
Welbeck St
New Cavendish St
Queen Anne St
Bulstrode St
Bentinck St
Tayer St
Hinde St
Mandeville Pl
James St
Workshop Coffee (p70)
Henrietta Pl
Marylebone L
MANCHESTER SQUARE

Daunt Books 4
Skandium 5
La Fromagerie 6
Moxon St
Aybrook St
Tapa Room at The Providores 10

MARYLEBONE

Fitzhardinge St
Wigmore St
PORTMAN SQUARE
George St
Montague St
Upper Berkeley St
Seymour St
Bryanston St
Portman S
Great Cumberland Pl

8 Dinings

Ⓤ Baker St
Bakerloo, Jubilee, Circle, Hammersmith & City, Metropolitan

Ⓤ Marylebone
Bakerloo

PAGE 26   MAYFAIR & MARYLEBONE

▲ SOHO (PAGE 10)

Oxford Circus
Bakerloo, Central, Victoria

Carnaby St
Kingly St
Beak St
Warwick St

Great Marlborough St
Princess St
Hanover St
Maddox St
Regent St
Savile Row
Mill St
11 Sketch
St George St
Conduit St
Clifford St
Vigo St
Burlington Gdns
Burlington Arcade
Royal Academy of Arts **3**

Jermyn St
White Cube (p55)
Duke St St James's
Berry Bros & Rudd **7**

ood Pl
HANOVER SQUARE
Hanover Square

w Bond St
12 Claridges Bar
1 Taylor St Baristas
9 Umu
Grafton St
Old Bond St
Dover Street Market
Albemarle St
Dover St
Berkeley St

St James's St
The Westbury
2

Piccadilly
ST JAMES'S

S Molton Lane
Davies St
Brook St
Bourdon St
Bruton Pl
Bruton St
BERKELEY SQUARE
Stratton St
Green Park
Jubilee, Piccadilly, Victoria

rt St
y St

Grosvenor St
MAYFAIR
Farm St
Hay's Mews
Charles St
Queen St
Bolton St
Half Moon St
GREEN PARK

udley St
GROSVENOR SQUARE
S Audley St
Chesterfield Hill
Ch'field St
Curzon Cinema (p22)
Curzon St
Shepherd St
Piccadilly

Waverton St
Hertford St
Brick St

Green St
Upper Brook St
Culross St
Upper Grosvenor St
Mount St
South St
Tilney St
Deanery St
Park Lane

Park Lane

HYDE PARK

200 metres

N

Mews Café
Taylor St Baristas

① 22 Brooks Mews, between Davies St and Avery Row
+44 20 7629 3163
taylor-st.com
⊖ ⊖ Bond Street
Closed Sat/Sun. Mon-Fri 8am-5pm.

In highbrow, clubby Mayfair it can be difficult to come across a standout espresso. Taylor St Baristas bucks this trend, with the help of a sleek La Marzocco Linea at their inviting Brooks Mews location. The café's crafted signature "rogue coffee" blend is joined by a delightful host of sandwiches, soups and cakes, as well as English apple and pear juices.

Piccadilly Splendour
The Wolseley

② 160 Piccadilly, at Arlington St
+44 20 7499 6996
thewolseley.com
⊖ ⊖ ⊖ Green Park
Open daily. Mon-Fri 7am-midnight; Sat 8am-midnight; Sun 8am-11pm.

In the 1920s, Wolseley Motors, now defunct, commissioned a grandiose car showroom on prestigious Piccadilly. While the car business did not fare all that well, The Wolseley was reborn in 2003 as one of the premier Continental-style café-restaurants in London. The bling of the setting and diverse clientele add to the celebratory exuberance of such delights as The Wolseley Champagne Tea, on offer daily.

Arts & Design Highlight

Royal Academy of Art

3 Burlington House, Piccadilly, between Old Bond St and Sackville St
+44 20 7300 8000
royalacademy.org.uk
⊖⊖⊖ Green Park, ⊖⊖ Piccadilly Circus
Open daily. Sun-Thu 10am-6pm; Fri 10am-midnight; Sat 9am-midnight. Admission £14.

Founded by George III in 1768, the Royal Academy's original members, consisting of artists and architects, were determined to form a centre dedicated to the achievement of professional standing for those fields in Britain. Today, the Royal Academy continues to enjoy its status as one of the premier sites in the UK for art exhibitions, including of the contemporary variety. Originally located in Somerset House (p16), its current, no less grandiose setting on Piccadilly adds to the splendour of the endeavour.

Edwardian Bookshop

Daunt Books

4 83 Marylebone High St, between Paddington St and Moxon St
+44 20 7224 2295
dauntbooks.com
⊖⊖⊖⊖⊖ Baker Street
Open daily. Mon-Sat 9am-7.30pm; Sun 11am-6pm.

Housed in an elegant Edwardian building and replete with a vast selection of books spanning the globe, Daunt Books is a Marylebone Village classic. Distributed over three floors, titles include fiction, non-fiction and an extensive range of travel writing. Browse the shelves, pick up a couple of paperbacks, and head over to the Marylebone branch of Nordic Bakery (p13) to lose yourself in some fiction, cinnamon bun and coffee.

Skandinavian Design

Skandium

⑤ 88 Marylebone High St, between Paddington St and Moxon St
+44 20 7935 2077
skandium.com
⊖⊖⊖⊖⊖ Baker Street
Open daily. Mon-Wed 10am-6.30pm; Thu 10am-7pm; Fri/Sat 10am-6.30pm; Sun 11am-5pm.

Skandium does not seem too far off from its aim of being the best retailer of Scandinavian design and furniture in the world. Founded by a Finn, a Swede and a Dane, all involved in the design industry in some capacity, the store is a haven of Nordic clean lines, soft wood and gorgeous textiles. To add to the authenticity, you will surely hear Swedish being spoken on Marylebone High Street, as the neighbourhood has long been a favourite of expat Swedes living in the British capital.

Cheesemonger

La Fromagerie

⑥ 2-6 Moxon St, between Cramer St and Marylebone High St
+44 20 7935 0341
lafromagerie.co.uk
⊖⊖⊖⊖⊖ Baker Street
Open daily. Mon-Fri 8am-7.30pm; Sat 9am-7pm; Sun 10am-6pm.

La Fromagerie is an urban hideaway in the heart of picturesque Marylebone Village. Serving as both one of Britain's premier cheese retailers and a full service tasting café, the locale offers a smart set of wine and cheese pairing menus to be enjoyed at its rustic communal table. Breakfast, lunch and afternoon tea are all on offer; or you could just swing by for some stilton and a bottle of Vilmart to be enjoyed as a picnic in one of the nearby parks.

Centuries of Wine Trading

Berry Bros. & Rudd

(7) 3 St James's St, at Pall Mall
+44 800 280 2440
bbr.com
🚇🚇🚇 Green Park
Closed Sun. Mon-Fri 10am-6pm; Sat 10am-5pm.

Britain's oldest wine and spirit merchant is still managed by the same families that established the venture three hundred years ago. Once the purveyor of choice to the burgeoning London coffee shop scene, as well as to the British Royal Family during the reign of King George III, Berry Brothers is also renowned for having weighed many of its customers, including Lord Byron, on its giant coffee scales. This illustrious history is more than matched by the vast and highly curated selection of wines and spirits on offer at the historic St James shop.

Japanese Tapas

Dinings

(8) 22 Harcourt St, between Old Marylebone Rd and Seymour Pl
+44 20 7723 0666
dinings.co.uk
🚇🚇🚇 Edgware Road,
🚇 Marylebone
Closed Sun. Lunch Mon-Sat noon-2.30pm. Dinner Mon-Sat 6pm-10.30pm.

Fusing traditional Japanese small plates with elements from other cuisines, Dinings is a high level izakaya-style gem. The restaurant's cosy banquettes allow for relaxed conversation over green tea, while course upon course of the freshest sushi and other Japanese treats unfold. Seared Scottish salmon sashimi topped with caviar, *wagyu* beef with porcini *ponzu* and fresh water eel and foie gras *donburi* are but a smattering of the gems concocted by Dinings' innovative kitchen.

Kyoto-Style Restaurant

Umu

9 14-16 Bruton Pl, off Bruton St
+44 20 7499 8881
umurestaurant.com
⊖⊖ Bond Street, ⊖⊖⊖ Green
Park
Closed Sun. Lunch Mon-Fri noon-
2.30pm. Dinner Mon-Sat 6pm-11pm.

The UK's only Kyoto-style Japanese
restaurant, Umu is as polished
and refined as its Mayfair mews
location. Each dish is meticulously
prepared and the fish could not
be fresher. Enjoy an intricate bento
box, including sashimi and a grilled
fish for lunch or treat yourself to a
stellar dinner with such delicacies
as tender *wagyu*, *toro* and *uni*. Try a
full-blown *kaiseki* menu to tantalize
the palate for hours on end. The
decor is modern-elegant with soft
lighting, polished wood and warm
toned accents.

Auckland Meets Marylebone

Tapa Room at The Providores

10 109 Marylebone High St, between
St Vincent St and Moxon St
+44 20 7935 6175
theprovidores.co.uk
⊖⊖⊖⊖ Baker Street, ⊖⊖ Bond
Street
Open daily. Breakfast Mon-Fri
9am-11.30am. Tapas Mon-Fri noon-
10.30pm. Brunch Sat/Sun 10am-
3pm. Dinner Sat 4pm-10.30pm; Sun
4pm-10pm.

An exciting fusion restaurant
specializing in small dishes and
wine, The Tapa Room offers an
unusually vast oenological selection
originating from New Zealand's
ten major wine regions. The
restaurant's innovative culinary
approach is complemented by an
equally strong coffee culture. Tapa
is named after the Pacific decorative
rug adorning the space's most
prominent wall.

Stylish Mayfair

Sketch

(11) 9 Conduit St, between Savile Row and Regent St
+44 20 7659 4500
sketch.uk.com
⊖⊖⊖ Oxford Circus
The Gallery: Open daily 6.30pm-2am. The Parlour: Closed Sun; Mon-Fri 8am-2am; Sat 10am-2am.

Divided into five flamboyantly decorated dining rooms and bars, Sketch is more of an experience than a restaurant. From decadent afternoon tea at the front room Parlour to a multi-course tasting menu at the Michelin starred Lecture Room, the venue caters to every whim. The Gallery, Sketch's brasserie, offers an ever-changing set of giant video images created by emerging artists to complement your French inspired meal. The bathrooms upstairs, consisting of retro-futuristic giant individual egg-like pods, are otherworldly.

Classic Drinks

Claridges Bar

(12) 49 Brook St, at Davies St
+44 20 7629 8860
claridges.co.uk
⊖⊖ Bond Street
Open daily. Mon-Sat noon-1am; Sun noon-midnight.

A quintessential English classic, refined, elegant and understated, a cocktail at Claridges Bar is a must. The original art deco features, including red leather banquettes, are scrupulously maintained. The unfussy luxury of the establishment pairs perfectly with one of London's most extensive champagne lists.

Notting Hill & the West
—Leafy London Ideal

Notting Hill comes closest to the London ideal sought by visitors and Londoners alike: well-kept Victorian townhouses, colourful mews and expansive private communal gardens. The neighbourhood is a vibrant, artistic, and still fairly mixed community centred on the picturesque Portobello Road street market.

The hill near the *Nutting-barns* manor was largely rural until the early 19th century when local landlords laid out plans for a fashionable suburb to capitalize on London's westward expansion. However, as middle class households ceased to employ servants in the first half of the 20th century, the large Notting Hill houses lost their market, and by the late 1950s many buildings had turned into down-market slums. The area was one of the few London neighbourhoods where Afro-Caribbean immigrants could find housing in postwar London. Subsequent attempts at "urban renewal" have left their mark on the neighbourhood, most notably Ernő Goldfinger's (also see p94) famously stark Trellick Tower. Notting Hill was rediscovered by the middle classes in the 1980s and developed into the urban idyll so famously portrayed in the eponymous 1999 film.

Today no less gentrified than other parts of Kensington and Chelsea, Notting Hill has maintained some of its social variety and artistic affinity. A short walk from the imposing and elegant white townhouses near Notting Hill Gate, Westbourne Grove and Ledbury Road have developed a reputation for their upmarket boutiques and eateries. Portobello Road, home to the famous Portobello Market, leads to the neighbourhood's edgier parts at the bottom of the hill. Further beyond, North Kensington's Golborne Road still exudes the neighbourhood's artistic and immigrant spirit.

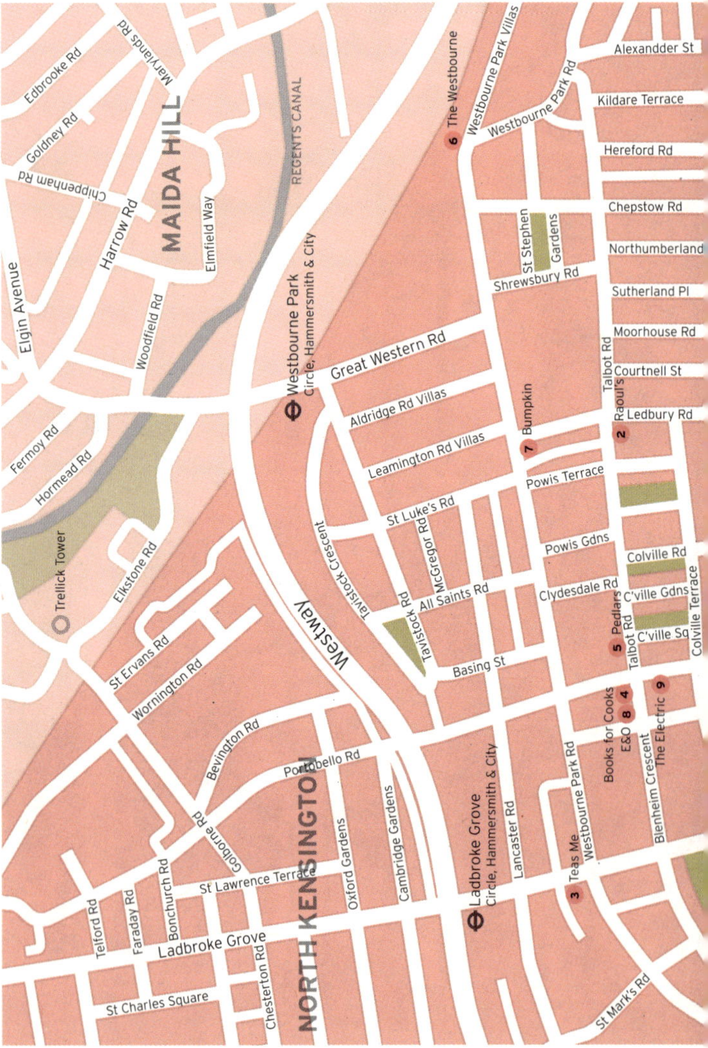

Edbrooke Rd
Goldney Rd
Chippenham Rd
Harrow Rd
Marylands Rd
Elmfield Way
MAIDA HILL
REGENTS CANAL
Woodfield Rd
Elgin Avenue
Fernroy Rd
Hormead Rd
Eikstone Rd
Trellick Tower
St Ervans Rd
Wornington Rd
Bevington Rd
Colborne Rd
Portobello Rd
Telford Rd
Faraday Rd
Bonchurch Rd
St Lawrence Terrace
Oxford Gardens
Cambridge Gardens
Chesterton Rd
Ladbroke Grove
St Charles Square
NORTH KENSINGTON
Ladbroke Grove
Circle, Hammersmith & City
Lancaster Rd
Teas Me 3
Westbourne Park Rd
Blenheim Crescent
The Electric 9
Books for Cooks
E&O 8 4
Westway
Tavistock Crescent
Westbourne Park
Circle, Hammersmith & City
Great Western Rd
Aldridge Rd Villas
Leamington Rd Villas
St Luke's Rd
All Saints Rd
Tavistock Rd
St McGregor Rd
Basing St
Clydesdale Rd
Powis Gdns
Powis Terrace
Bumpkin
7
Raoul's
Talbot Rd
Ledbury Rd 2
Courtnell St
Moorhouse Rd
Sutherland Pl
Northumberland
Chepstow Rd
Hereford Rd
Kildare Terrace
Alexandder St
Westbourne Park Villas
Westbourne Park Rd
The Westbourne 6
St Stephen Gardens
Shrewsbury Rd
C'ville Gdns
Colville Rd
Colville Terrace
C'ville Sq
Talbot Rd
Padliers 5

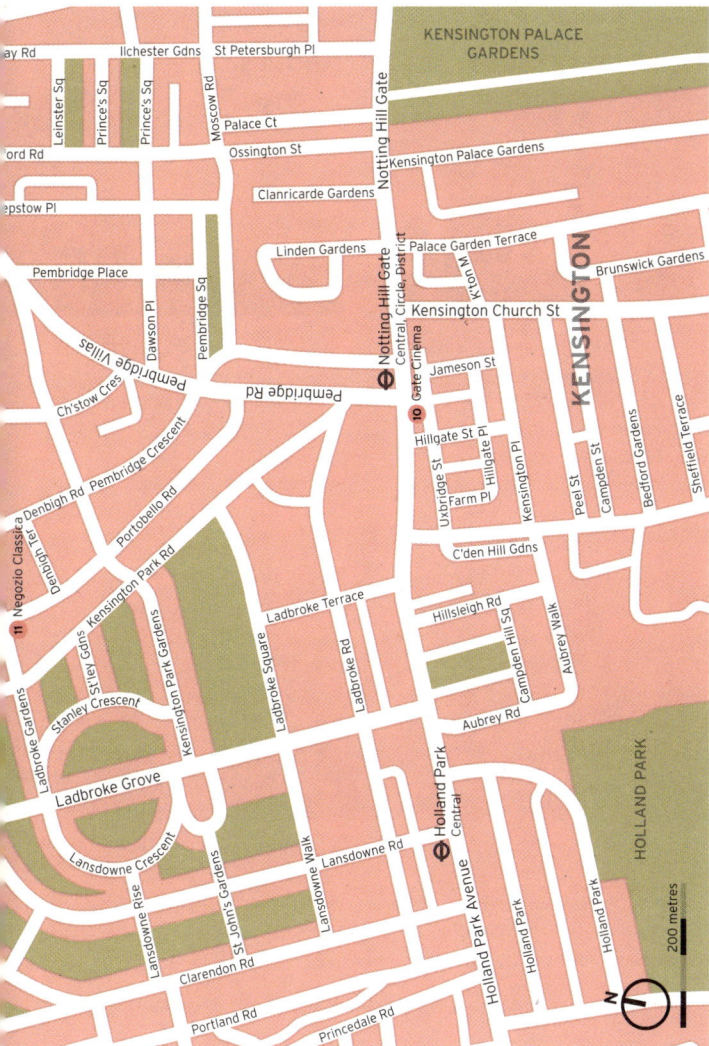

KENSINGTON PALACE GARDENS

ay Rd

Ilchester Gdns   St Petersburgh Pl

Leinster Sq

Prince's Sq

Prince's Sq

Moscow Rd

Palace Ct

Ossington St

ford Rd

Notting Hill Gate

Kensington Palace Gardens

epstow Pl

Clanricarde Gardens

Pembroke Place

Linden Gardens

Palace Garden Terrace

Pembridge Sq

Dawson Pl

Pembridge Villas

Notting Hill Gate
Central, Circle, District

K'ton M

Brunswick Gardens

KENSINGTON

Ch'stow Cres

Pembridge Rd

Kensington Church St

Pembridge Crescent

Gate Cinema

Jameson St

Denbigh Rd

Denbigh Ter

Portobello Rd

Hillgate St

Uxbridge St

Hillgate Pl

Kensington Pl

Peel St

Campden St

Bedford Gardens

Sheffield Terrace

Farm Pl

11 Negozio Classica

Ladbroke Gardens

St'ley Gdns

Stanley Crescent

Kensington Park Rd

Kensington Park Gardens

Ladbroke Terrace

Ladbroke Square

Ladbroke Rd

C'den Hill Gdns

Hillsleigh Rd

Campden Hill Sq

Aubrey Walk

Ladbroke Grove

Lansdowne Crescent

Lansdowne Rise

St John's Gardens

Lansdowne Walk

Lansdowne Rd

Aubrey Rd

Holland Park
Central

HOLLAND PARK

Clarendon Rd

Portland Rd

Princedale Rd

Holland Park Avenue

Holland Park

Holland Park

Holland Park

200 metres

N

Notting Hill Guesthouse
The Main House

1 6 Colville Rd, between Lonsdale Rd and Westbourne Grove
+44 20 7221 9691
themainhouse.co.uk
⊖⊖⊖ Notting Hill Gate
Rooms from £55 per person per night incl. tax; excl. breakfast, available at nearby Tom's Deli.

Situated just around the corner from picture perfect Westbourne Grove and its throng of stylish shops, The Main House affords the visitor a genuine taste of Notting Hill living. Each guest occupies an en-suite floor of the beautifully appointed Victorian house and can enjoy complimentary morning coffee or tea and the paper— served in the room or on the balcony. The choice of restaurants, bars and entertainment within walking distance of the House is astounding and the setting is utterly charming.

Notting Hill Brunch
Raoul's

2 105-107 Talbot Rd, between Powis Terrace and Ledbury Rd
+44 20 7229 2400
raoulsgourmet.com
⊖⊖ Westbourne Park,
⊖⊖⊖ Notting Hill Gate
Open daily. Mon-Sat 8.30am-11pm; Sun 9am-7pm.

A Notting Hill brunch classic, Raoul's is a people watching paradise with a heated outside terrace to match. Combining Mediterranean cuisine with more classic brunch items, the menu is versatile around the clock. Cheerful yellow accents highlighting the blonde wooden tables and oversized mirrors make for a soothing and light ambiance. For those who prefer brunch to spill into evening cocktails, a lower ground floor bar opens up at night.

Neighbourhood Café

Teas Me

③ 129a Ladbroke Grove, at Ladbroke Crescent
+44 20 7729 5577
⊖⊖ Ladbroke Grove
Open daily. Mon-Sat 7.30am-6pm;
Sun 10am-5pm.

In a nod to the neighbourhood's lesser known Portuguese influences, Teas Me serves an excellent breakfast/brunch as well as an array of delectable homemade cakes, teas and coffees. The ambiance is warm, refined and convivial, and a newspaper strewn common table is meticulously decorated with fresh flowers. On warmer days tables are also set outside on Ladbroke Crescent, a picturesque cul-de-sac just off Ladbroke Grove.

Foodie Classic

Books for Cooks

④ 4 Blenheim Crescent, between Kensington Park Rd and Portobello Rd
+44 20 7221 1992
booksforcooks.com
⊖⊖ Ladbroke Grove
Closed Mon/Sun. Tue-Sat 10am-6pm.

Books for Cooks offers an astonishing selection of its eponymous materials in a quaint and festive shop on attractive Blenheim Crescent. While cooking classes are held upstairs, new additions to the cookbook range are given a test run in the kitchen, which doubles as an in-house café. Comfy couches in such a pleasant setting make it tempting to while away an afternoon in the company of so many distinguished books and *friandises*.

Vintage Design
Pedlars

⑤ 128 Talbot Rd, between Portobello Road and Colville Square
+44 20 7727 7799
pedlars.co.uk
⊖⊖ Ladbroke Grove
Open daily. Mon-Sat 10am-6pm; Sun noon-6pm.

Located next door to the famous Rough Trade record shop, Pedlar's sells a staggering array of vintage and original items, including clocks, maps, posters, prints, books, curiosities and furniture, most with a strong infusion of UK flavour. The space is at once cosy and whimsical, giving off an Alice in Wonderland-like serendipitous vibe. The ideal place to snap up a gift or two…for oneself.

Notting Hill Public House
The Westbourne

⑥ 101 Westbourne Park Villas, at Westbourne Park Rd
+44 20 7221 1332
thewestbourne.com
⊖⊖ Royal Oak
Open daily. Mon-Thu 4.30pm-11pm; Fri/Sat 11am-11pm; Sun noon-10.30pm. Dinner Mon-Sat 6.30pm-10.15pm; Sun 6.30pm-9.30pm.

An ever-popular gastropub on a Notting Hill corner bursting with wild flowers, The Westbourne serves a constantly changing menu chiselled out of locally sourced produce in a jovial setting. A good variety of wines and beers are on offer, and the Westbourne's generous terrace is one of London's best. For those wanting to stay inside during the colder months, the pub's interior is all warm tones and wood.

A Taste of Seasonal Britain

Bumpkin

7 209 Westbourne Park Rd, at
Ledbury Rd
+44 20 7243 9818
bumpkinuk.com
🚇 Westbourne Park
Open daily. Mon-Fri 11am-11pm; Sat/
Sun 9am-11pm.

Seasonal British fare is served with
aplomb at this rustic-urban Notting
Hill restaurant. The recipient of a
soil award for sustainable practices,
Bumpkin sources the freshest
organic ingredients from across
the British Isles. A host of British
ciders, ales, beers, English wines
and bespoke British cocktails are
also on offer to add merriment to a
delightful meal.

Notting Hill Cool

E&O

8 14 Blenheim Crescent, at
Kensington Park Rd
+44 20 7229 5454
rickerrestaurants.com
🚇 Ladbroke Grove
Open daily. Lunch Mon-Fri noon-
3pm. Dinner Mon-Fri 6pm-11pm;
Sat noon-11pm; Sunday 12.30pm-
10.30pm. Bar open one hour longer.

On a bijou corner of Blenheim
Crescent, E&O serves nouveau
pan-Asian cuisine in a modern,
urbane setting. Dishes are artfully
displayed and are matched by the
high calibre of the wine and drinks
list. Australian ownership makes for
a refreshingly laid back experience.
The front bar and outdoor benches
are stellar spots to quaff a cocktail
or two.

Brasserie & Boutique Cinema

The Electric

9 191 Portobello Rd, between
Blenheim and Elgin Crescents
+44 20 7908 9696
electricbrasserie.com
⊖ Ladbroke Grove,
⊖⊖⊖ Notting Hill Gate
Open daily. Mon-Wed 8am-midnight;
Thu-Sat 8am-1am; Sun 8am-11pm.
Screenings daily. Refer to website
for showtimes. Tickets £15.

London's most unusual and
luxurious film house is happily
combined with one of Notting Hill's
most successful brasseries. The
Electric Cinema comes replete with
oversized chairs, plush footrests
and side tables on which to rest
your glass of champagne and
mixed olives. Those seeking more
intimacy can opt for a double
love seat. Combine the show with
some classic Continental fare at the
adjoining brasserie and enjoy the
spectacle of Portobello Road as it
unfolds before your eyes.

Independent Film

Gate Cinema

10 87 Notting Hill Gate,
at Pembridge Rd
+44 871 902 5731
picturehouses.co.uk
⊖⊖⊖ Notting Hill Gate
Screenings daily. Refer to website
for showtimes. Tickets £12.50.

A pathbreaking arthouse cinema
with a long and fascinating history,
the Gate remains one of the best
film houses in London. Located in
an Edwardian building and former
hotel of "dubious reputation",
the then Electric Palace theatre
opened its doors in 1911. Surviving
multiple setbacks, including the
advent of television at a time when
most cinemas were converting
into bingo parlours, The Gate is
a testament to the allure of the
silver screen. The cinema's front bar
allows for some prime Notting Hill
Gate streetscape watching.

Italian Wine Bar

Negozio Classica

11 283 Westbourne Grove,
at Portobello Rd
+44 20 7034 0005
negozioclassica.co.uk
⊖⊖⊖ Notting Hill Gate
Open daily. Mon-Thu 3.30pm-
midnight; Fri/Sun 10am-midnight;
Sat 9am-midnight.

A sleek Italian wine bar and café,
Negozio Classica offers the best
of Italy in the heart of Notting Hill.
The bar, comfy living room chairs
and discreet fireplaces conjure the
luxury of a Milanese lounge. Wines
can be paired with an epicurean
selection of cheeses and cured
meats and many of the items are
also available to purchase for later
consumption. During the day,
Negozio Classica lends itself very
well to the rapturous combination
of espresso and newspaper.

Royal Albert Hall

Kensington Gore

Jay Mews

Prince Consort Rd

Kensington Gate

Palace Gate

De Vere Gardens

Calendar Rd

Queen's Gate

Prince Gdns

Ennismore Gnds

Exhibition Rd

Ayrton Rd

Princes Gardens

Queen's Gate Terrace

Gore St

Petersham Pl

Elvaston Pl

Gloucester Rd

Imperial College Rd

Queens Gate Pl

Queen's Gate Gardens

Museum Lane

KENSINGTON

Southwell Gdns

Natural History Museum

13 V&A Museum

Thurloe Pl

Cromwell Rd

Cromwell Pl

Thurloe Pl

Thurloe St

Thurloe Sq

Alexander Pl

Stanhope Gdns

Stanhope Gdns

Queen's Gate

Gloucester Rd
Piccadilly, District, Circle

Stanhope Gardens

Harringdon Rd

Pelham St

Thurloe St

South Kensington
Piccadilly, District, Circle

South Terrace

Pelham St

Glendover Pl

Pelham St

Gloucester Rd

Wetherby Pl

Clareville Grove

Clareville St

Manson Pl

Pelham Pl Crescent

Rosary Gardens

Old Brompton Rd

Bumpkin (p41)

Brechin Pl

Cranley Pl

Onslow Gardens

Sydney Pl

Elystan St

Lucan

Roland Gardens

Cranley Gardens

Onslow Gardens

Onslow Sq

Sumner Pl

Onslow Sq

Sydney St

Pond Pl

Bury Walk

Ixworth Pl

Foulis Terrace

Neville St

Selwood Terrace

Fulham Rd

Dovehouse St

Sydney's Grove

Stewart's Grove

Cale Pl

Tom's Kitchen **12**

St Luke's St

Evelyn Gardens

South Parade

Chelsea Sq

N

200 metres

HYDE PARK

South Carriage Drive

Kensington Rd

Knightsbridge

Rutland Gate

Trevor Pl

Trevor St

Raphael St

Harvey Nichols

Knightsbridge

Piccadilly

Wilton Pl

KNIGHTSBRIDGE

Montpelier Sq

Montpelier St

Montpelier Walk

Basil St

Pavilion Rd

Lowndes Sq

Kinnerton St

Wilton Crescent

Cheval Pl

Harrods

Hans Rd

Hans Crescent

Motcomb St

Wilton Ter

Belgrave Mews W

BELGRAVE SQUARE

Brompton Rd

Brompton Pl

Beaufort Gardens

Basil St

W Halkin St

Halkin St

Beauchamp Pl

Cadogan Pl

Belgrave Mews W

Yeoman's Row

Ovington Gardens

Walton St

Hans Pl

Hans St

Lowndes St

Chesham Pl

Lowndes Pl

Terrace

Pont St

Cadogan Sq

Cadogan Sq

Pavilion Rd

Sloane St

Cadogan Pl

Cadogan Lane

Chesham St

Lyall St

Eaton Pl

First St

Hasker St

Ovington St

Lennox Gdns

CHELSEA

BELGRAVIA

Eaton Sq

Mossop St

Denyer St

Milner St

Hasley St

Moore St

Cadogan Gate

Ellis St

Eaton Sq

Draycott Av

Rawlings St

Rosemoor St

Cadogan St

Draycott Ter

Cadogan Gdns

Gardens

Wilbraham Pl

Sloane Ter

Eaton Gate

South Eaton Pl

Sloane Av

Whitehead's Grove

Spirmont Pl

Elystan Pl

Bray Pl

Draycott Pl

Culford Gdns

Symons St

Sloane Square

Sloane Gardens

Bourne St

Caroline Ter

Eaton Terrace

Chester Row

Graham Terrace

Sloane Sq

District, Circle

Markham St

Bywater St

Tyron St

King's Rd

Cheltenham Ter

Walpole St

Lower Sloane St

Sloane Gardens

Holbein Pl

Ebury St

La Poule au Pot **14**

Pimlico Rd

Brunch in Chelsea
Tom's Kitchen

12 27 Cale St, between St Luke's St and Astell St, Chelsea
+44 20 7349 0202.
tomskitchen.co.uk
⊖⊖⊖ South Kensington
Open daily. Breakfast Mon-Fri 8am-11.45am; Sat/Sun 10am-1pm. Lunch Mon-Fri noon-3pm; Sat/Sun 1pm-3pm. Dinner Mon-Fri 6pm-11pm; Sat/Sun 6pm-10.30pm.

Tom Aiken's venture into more laid back waters is a buzzy all day brasserie dining spot, catering to the well-heeled Chelsea crowd. The menu reflects a modern and sustainable British spin on French brasserie dishes, including some rather un-Continental brunch classics, the likes of blueberry pancakes with maple syrup. An upstairs bar serves signature house cocktails, including the My Fruity Wife.

Design Heritage
V&A Museum

13 Cromwell Rd, at Thurloe Place, South Kensington
+44 20 7942 2000
vam.ac.uk
⊖⊖⊖ South Kensington
Open daily. Sat-Thu 10am-5.45pm; Fri 10am-10pm. Free admission.

A bastion of decorative arts and design, the Victoria & Albert Museum's sweeping collection of 4.5 million objects would be reason enough to visit, but the building's architecture provides motivation just as compelling. Founded in 1852, the museum's collection spans the globe and five thousand years of design. The V&A's focus is on practically used objects, rather than high art or research, thus offering fascinating insights into the visual history of the quotidian. Ever the trendsetter, the museum was the first in Britain to host a rock concert in 1973.

La Poule au Pot

14 231 Ebury St, between Bourne St and Eaton Terrace, Belgravia
+44 20 7730 7763
pouleaupot.co.uk
⊖⊖ Sloane Square
Open daily. Lunch Mon-Fri noon-2.30pm; Sat/Sun noon-4pm. Dinner Mon-Sat 6.45pm-11pm; Sun 6.45pm-10pm.

Located on Ebury Street in posh Belgravia, a stone's throw from Chelsea's upmarket Sloane Square, La Poule au Pot cooks up a rustic French storm in a setting to match. Authentic and low key, the restaurant's menu offers the full gamut of French fare, from *bouillabaisse* to *coq au vin* culminating in delectable deserts, including, of course, *tarte tatin*, and an extensive wine list. This is also a great spot to have a go at your French, as the waiters will happily address you in their native tongue.

Shoreditch & the East

—London's Cutting Edge

Only two decades ago Shoreditch was a wasteland of light industrial structures on the fringes of the City of London, the old Roman settlement and today's financial district. All this changed in the 1990s when the area around Hoxton Square turned into the epicentre of a thriving art scene. London's artistic centre of gravity has steadily moved eastwards ever since.

The East End, unlike London's western suburbs, did not see much planned development but grew as an impromptu response to London's breakneck expansion during the Industrial Revolution and the extension of the nearby docks. Spitalfields and Brick Lane in particular have been shaped by the waves of immigrants who lived there—Huguenots in the 17th century, Irish and Jewish, and more recently Bangladeshi. The narrow lanes of Jack the Ripper's 19th century East End fell victim to the air raids of the German Blitz during World War II, which turned swathes of terraces into rubble. The closure of London's docks in the 1980s added another setback, although this was partly offset by office developments that sprouted up at Canary Wharf in the 1990s.

The East End today has morphed into an interesting hotchpotch of its down-heeled past and its more buoyant present. The core of the former bohemian neighbourhood around Hoxton Square and Redchurch Street is now a mecca for trendy boutiques and upscale restaurants. The area near the Old Street roundabout is a centre of London's burgeoning tech start-up scene. To the south, Spitalfields Market has developed into an increasingly mainstream retail success story. Many artists have moved east to Bethnal Green which is still decidedly rough around the edges.

▲ BETHNAL GREEN (PAGE 52)

Thurtle St
Scawfell St
Dunloe St
Dawson St
Weymouth Terrace
Ravenscroft St
Brawn
Gosset St
Chiltor
Appleby St
Pearson St
Ormsby St
Diss St
Columbia Rd
Chambers St
Padbury Ct
Shacklewell St
Brick Lane
Geffrye Museum
Hoxton Overground
Dunloe St
Geffrye St
Cremer St
Gorsuch St
Pelter St
Gascoigne Pl
Swanfield St
Rochelle Canten
Rhoda St
Labour & Walt
Nazrul St
Long St
Austin St
Calvert Av
Rile St
Montclare St
Club Row
Hare Walk
Shenfield St
Stanway St
Union Walk
Waterson St
18 Jaguar Shoes
Hackney Rd
Navarre St
Camlet St
Old Nichol St
9 The Boundary
Redchurch St
Palissy St
12
Boundary St
Arnold
Circus
4
Kingsland Rd
Prufrock at Present (p69) Virginia Rd
Shoreditch High St
SHOREDITCH
Falkirk St
Hoxton St
Regan Way
Crondale St
HOXTON
Drysdale Rd
Hoxton St
Rivington St
Bateman's Row
New Inn Yard
Purcell St
Buckland St
Pitfield St
Fanshaw St
Bowling Green Walk Mundy St
HOXTON SQUARE
White Cube
5
Curtain Rd
Charlotte Rd
ordan Walk
Great Eastern St
New North Rd
Ashford St
Coronet St
Boot St
Old St
Phipp St
Ravey St
Willow St
Blackall St
Bevenden St
Haberdasher St
Butland St
Chart St
Charles Sq
Pitfield St
Singer St
14 Eyre Brothers
Luke St
Clere St
Murray Grove
Chart St
Corsham St
Brunswick Pl
Vince St
Cowper St
Leonard St
Epworth St Taylor St Baristas (p28)
Provost St
Nile St
Vestry St
East Rd
Cranwood St
Old St
Northern
Scrut
Rd
Britannia Walk
ld Westland
Old St
Mallow St
Featherstone St
▼ CLERKENWELL (PAGE 65)

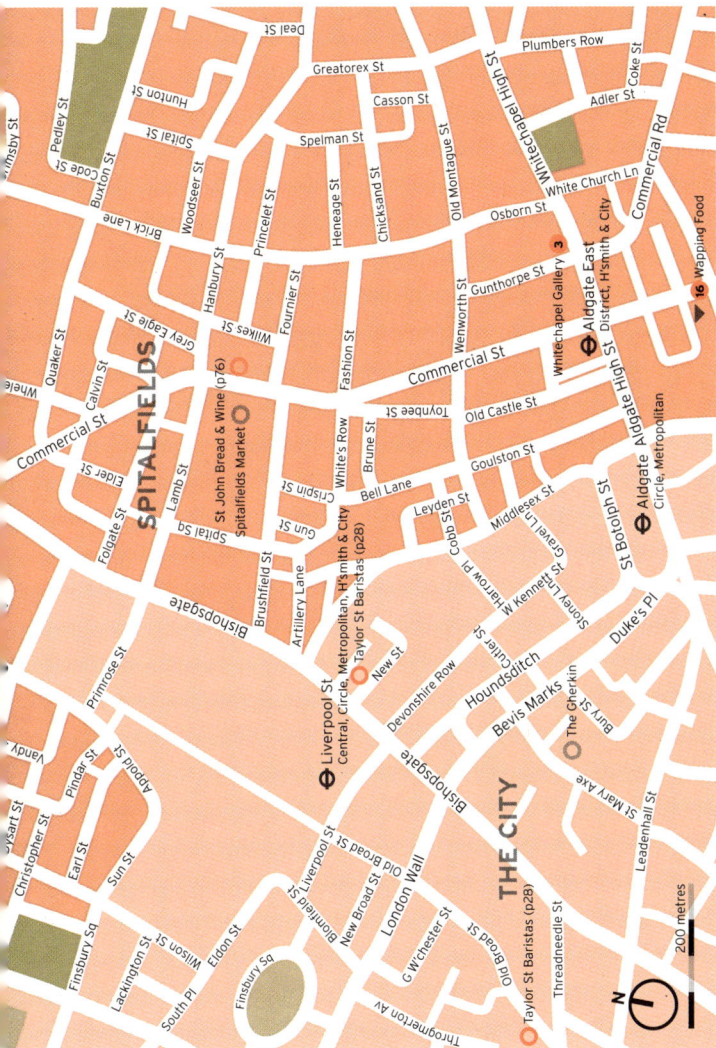

Deal St

Greatorex St

Plumbers Row

Hunton St

Casson St

Pedley St

Spital St

Spelman St

Whitechapel High St

Adler St

Code St

Woodseer St

Buxton St

Princelet St

Heneage St

Old Montague St

Coke St

Brick Lane

Hanbury St

Chicksand St

Osborn St

White Church Ln

Commercial Rd

Grey Eagle St

Fournier St

Wenworth St

Whitechapel Gallery **3**

Wapping Food

Quaker St

Wilkes St

Fashion St

Gunthorpe St

16

Calvin St

Commercial St

Commercial St

Elder St

St John Bread & Wine (p76)

White's Row

Toynbee St

Old Castle St

Aldgate East
District, H'smith & City

Folgate St

Lamb St

Spitalfields Market

Brune St

Goulston St

Aldgate
Circle, Metropolitan

SPITALFIELDS

Spital Sq

Bell Lane

Leyden St

Aldgate High St

St Botolph St

Brushfield St

Gun St

Crispin St

Cobb St

Middlesex St

Duke's Pl

Bishopsgate

Artillery Lane

Devonshire Row

Cutler St

Houndsditch

Gravel Lane

Stoney Ln

W Harrow Pl

W Kennett St

Liverpool St
Central, Circle, Metropolitan, H'smith & City

New St

Bevis Marks

The Gherkin

Taylor St Baristas (p28)

Primrose St

Bury St

St Mary Axe

Leadenhall St

Appold St

Pindar St

Sun St

Eldon St

Wilson St

London Wall

Old Broad St

Bishopsgate

THE CITY

Christopher St

Earl St

Lackington St

South Pl

Finsbury Sq

Liverpool St

New Broad St

Blomfield St

G W'chester St

Old Broad St

Threadneedle St

Finsbury Sq

Throgmerton Av

Taylor St Baristas (p28)

200 metres

N

Waterloo Gdns

Peary Pl

Globe Rd

Bonner Rd

Robinson Rd

Approach Rd

Russia Lane

Globe Rd

Burnham St

BETHNAL GREEN

Vicar's Close

Bistrotheque

10

Mowlem St

Vyner St

Wadeson St

Bishop's Way

Parmiter St

Peel Grove

Patriot Sq

Viajante

17

Victoria Park Sq

Old Ford Rd

Roman Rd

Bethnal Green
Central

Mare St

Andrews Rd

REGENTS CANAL

Cambridge Heath Rd

Clare St

Poyser St

Paradise Row

St Jude's Rd

Hollybush Gardens

C'bridge Cres

Centre St

Punderson's Gardens

Pott St

Minerva St

Elsworth St

Middleton St

Emma St

Temple St

Winkley St

Canrobert St

Wilmot St

Ada Pl

Pritchard's Rd

Claredale St

Sheldon Pl

Teesdale St

Maple St

Dove Row

Little Georgia

11

Teale St

Coate St

Mansford St

St Peter's Cl

Old Bethnal Green Rd

Bethnal Green Rd

Kay St

Hackney Rd

Nelson Gdns

Pollard St

Voss St

Derbyshire St

Audrey St

Goldsmith's Row

Pollard Row

Ivimey St

Florida St

Squirries St

Vallance Rd

Warner Pl

Durant St

Roberta St

Buckfast St

Baxendale St

Wimbolt St

Barnet Grove

Yorkton St

6

Columbia Rd

Barnet Grove

Quilter St

Queensbridge Rd

Bath Grove

Horatio St

Ezra St

Elwin St

Wellington Row

Turin St

Kent St

Scawfell St

Shipton St

Brawn

13

Gosset St

Thurtle Rd

Dunloe St

Dawson St

Ravenscroft St

Weymouth Terrace

▼ SHOREDITCH (PAGE 50)

200 metres

N

Shoreditch House Accommodation

Shoreditch Rooms

① Ebor St, between Bethnal Green
Rd and Redchurch St
+44 20 7739 5040
shoreditchhouse.com
⊖⊖⊖⊖ Liverpool Street
Doubles from £225 incl. tax (Tiny
rooms from £205 incl. tax); excl.
breakfast, available in-house.

Shoreditch House is the East End
offshoot of Soho House, the global
members' club. The Shoreditch
Rooms are open to non-members.
Accommodation is spread over
five floors of pleasantly airy rooms
with vintage touches and sweeping
views of the City or of charming
Ebor Street. Smack in the middle
of the East End's most vibrant
neighbourhood, this is the place
to be for a taste of contemporary
London and some pampering,
facilitated by the presence of the
on-site Cowshed Spa and Gym.

New Zealand Import

Allpress

② 58 Redchurch St, at Club Row
+44 20 7749 1780
uk.allpressespresso.com
⊖⊖⊖⊖ Liverpool Street
Open daily. Mon-Fri 8am-5pm; Sat/
Sun 9am-5pm.

A New Zealand import, Allpress
roasts its signature Costa Rican
beans on-premise and executes
each flavourful cup meticulously.
Located on a picturesque and
vibrant corner of Redchurch Street,
the café's enormous windows allow
for some in-depth people watching
while you sip away at your espresso.
For an invigorating afternoon, why
not combine your caffeination
at Allpress with a stroll around
Shoreditch and some shopping
at Labour & Wait (p56) across the
street.

East End Pioneer

Whitechapel Gallery

3 77-82 Whitechapel High St, at Gunthorpe St
+44 20 7522 7888
whitechapelgallery.org
⊖ ⊖ Aldgate East, ⊖ ⊖ Aldgate
Closed Mon. Fri-Wed 11am-6pm; Thu 11am-9pm. Free admission.

The Whitechapel Gallery focuses on modern and contemporary art in one of London's rough-around-the-edges neighbourhoods. In 1956, the gallery's "This Is Tomorrow" exhibition famously launched Pop Art as a popular genre. Thanks to the London Open, its open-submission show running since 1936, Whitechapel has catapulted the careers of several renowned artists, including sculptor Anish Kapoor. The gallery's downstairs dining room is minimalist chic, while the upstairs café with its thick wooden planks offers fresh and sprightly lunch specials.

London Homes throughout History

Geffrye Museum

4 136 Kingsland Rd, between Cremer St and Pearson St
+44 20 7739 9893
geffrye-museum.org.uk
⊖ Old Street
Closed Mon. Tue-Sat 10am-5pm; Sun noon-5pm. Free admission.

The Geffrye Museum affords visitors a fascinating glimpse into the history of England's changing domestic interior design from the 1600s to the present. A series of eleven rooms serves to illustrate the different periods with typical furnishing, ornaments and wallpaper, supplemented by illuminating explanatory notes. In addition, the museum showcases four wildly varying English gardens, each one representing horticultural styles of the past four centuries.

Cutting Edge Hoxton
White Cube

5 48 Hoxton Square, at Rufus St
+44 20 7930 5373
whitecube.com
⊖ Old Street
Closed Sun/Mon. Tue-Sat 10am-6pm.

Featuring work by cutting edge and controversial contemporary artists in a 1920s light industrial cubic space, White Cube makes for an electric stop-off on the Shoreditch circuit. When it opened in 2000, the gallery's unusual frosted white glass cube structure overlooking trendy Hoxton Square became synonymous with the area's revival, which had started in the 1990s. Damian Hirst's notorious diamond skull (For the Love of God) was exhibited here in the 2007 show Beyond Belief.

Picturesque East End
Columbia Road

6 Columbia Rd, between Gosset St and Hackney Rd
columbiaroad.info
⊖ Bethnal Green
Flower Market: Sun 8am-3pm.

Columbia Road is a quaint high street of colourful low-rise terraced houses and small-scale retail behind intricate shop fronts—a taste of the old East End in an area that is otherwise dominated by slab concrete housing estates. On Sundays, the street turns into a sea of colour during the Columbia Road Flower Market. Here, specialist traders hawk the entire gamut from cut flowers to exotic offerings such as banana trees.

Design Classics for the Home
Labour & Wait

🔅 85 Redchurch St, between
Chance St and Club Row
+44 20 7729 6253
labourandwait.co.uk
⊖⊖⊖⊖ Liverpool Street
Closed Mon. Tue-Sun 11am-6pm.

Having grown weary of fast
fashion's ravages, menswear design
veterans Rachel Wythe-Moran
and Simon Watkins developed
the concept for Labour & Wait.
With a focus on craftsmanship and
timeless design, the shop's highly
curated selection of functional
objects never fails to delight. From
Welsh blankets to English pottery,
vintage flasks and Japanese enamel
teapots joyfully displayed in the
shop's inviting setting; you will be
sure to unearth a treasure or two.

Treasure Cove
Cheshire Street

🔅 Cheshire St, between Brick Lane
and St Matthew's Row
⊖⊖⊖⊖ Liverpool Street
Beach London: open daily 10am-
6pm.

Cheshire Street, an inconspicuous
side street off popular Brick Lane,
has developed into a haven of
creative talent and small-scale retail.
In contrast to East London's housing
estates and rows of uninterrupted
brick houses, Cheshire Street is
dotted with colourfully painted
front panels. Drop by Beach London
(at number 20), a small gallery, print
shop, bookstore and café, to get a
glimpse of the latest in London's art
and illustration scene and to refuel
with a macchiato. On select dates
in December the street cracks open
the mulled wine and mince pies,
and shops stay open late to partake
in the festivities.

Hotel, Restaurant & Rooftop Bar

The Boundary

9 2-4 Boundary St, at Redchurch St
+44 20 7729 1051
theboundary.co.uk
Liverpool Street
Open daily. Albion: 8am-11pm.
Rooftop: noon-9.30pm. Lunch noon-
4pm. Dinner 5.30pm-8.30pm.

The slick and contemporary
Boundary Project by British design
icon Terence Conran includes three
restaurants, a hotel and a gallery
space, but the jewel in the crown
is surely the gorgeous outdoor
rooftop bar and grill, complete with
stunning views of London's East
End and the City. The Albion Café
on the ground floor serves top of
the line British fare, some of which it
also sells retail in its in-house shop.

Bethnal Green Pizzazz

Bistrotheque

10 23-27 Wadeson St, between
Cambridge Heath Rd and Mowlem St
+44 20 8983 7900
bistrotheque.com
Bethnal Green
Open daily. Dinner Sun-Thu 6.30pm-
10.30pm; Fri/Sat 6.30pm-11pm.
Brunch Sat/Sun 11am-4pm.

Housed in an industrial space in
edgy Bethnal Green, Bistrotheque's
main restaurant serves up a fanciful
full brunch and English inspired
selection for dinner, backed up by
a host of excellent regional French
wines. The space's other highlights
include a cabaret room, complete
with drag queen performances, and
the cosy Oak Room bar.

A Taste of the East
Little Georgia

11 87 Goldsmith's Row, at Audrey St
+44 20 7739 8154
littlegeorgia.co.uk
⊖ Bethnal Green
Open daily. Café Mon-Fri 8.30am-
6pm; Sat/Sun 9am-6pm. Dinner
Tue-Sun 7pm-late.

Little Georgia brings a taste of the
East to East London. Decorated
with Georgian photography
and artefacts, the cosy space is
welcoming at any time of day. The
menu is chock full of scrumptious
dishes, including perfectly seasoned
lamb *kababi* and a hot rendition of
borscht. To top it off, Little Georgia
supports customer's oenological
independence by operating a no-
corkage BYOB policy.

Shoreditch Cuisine
Rochelle Canteen

12 Arnold Circus, between Rochelle
St and Club Row
+44 20 7729 5677
arnoldandhenderson.com
⊖⊖⊖⊖ Liverpool Street
Closed Sat/Sun. Breakfast Mon-Fri
9am-noon. Lunch noon-3pm. Tea
3pm-4.30pm.

Delicious, fresh lunches are served
on weekdays in this urban oasis
hidden in a Victorian school yard.
Converted from a former bike shed,
Rochelle Canteen's wide panel glass
doors are opened on warm days,
allowing the restaurant to spill into
the picturesque surrounding yard.
The establishment is the creation
of serial caterers and restaurateurs
Arnold & Henderson.

Columbia Road French

Brawn

13 49 Columbia Rd, at Ravenscroft St
+44 20 7729 5692
brawn.co
⊖ Bethnal Green
Open daily. Lunch Thu-Sat noon-3pm; Sun set lunch noon-4pm.
Dinner Mon-Sat 6pm-11pm.

Decked out in warm wood and exuding comfort, Brawn specializes in locally sourced delicacies in a wonderfully unfussy setting. The highlight of Columbia Road's many culinary treasures, a meal at Brawn can include such divergent delights as Scottish langoustine, braised rabbit leg, soft polenta and *gremalata*, and the rather more unusual sounding snails, oxtail and salsify pie. Brawn's predominantly French list of sustainable, organic and biodynamic wines is particularly satisfying.

Iberian Flair

Eyre Brothers

14 70 Leonard St, between Paul St and Ravey St
+44 20 7613 5346
eyrebrothers.co.uk
⊖ Old Street
Closed Sun. Lunch Mon-Fri noon-3pm. Dinner Mon-Fri 6.30pm-10.45pm; Sat 7pm-10.45pm.

Arguably London's best Iberian restaurant, Eyre Brothers melds culinary artistry with a cultivated, contemporary decor. Every element, from the splash of green olive oil bursting with flavor to the stellar wine list, evokes pure pleasure. Muted lighting, modernist wood panelling, tasteful artwork and a buzzing bar add to the restaurant's infinite appeal; but its culinary might is certainly worth multiple visits in of itself.

French Fantaisie

Les Trois Garçons

15 1 Club Row, at Bethnal Green Road
+44 20 7613 1924
lestroisgarcons.com
🚇🚇🚇🚇 Liverpool Street
Closed Sun. Lunch Mon-Fri noon-2.30pm. Dinner Mon-Sat 6pm-10.30pm.

In the year 2000, the trois garçons Hassan, Michel and Stefan, from Malaysia, France and Sweden respectively, unveiled an over-the-top baroque-chic French restaurant in the former Victorian pub they had already inhabited for four years. Les Trois Garçons takes the Gallic notion of *fantaisie* to new heights. The eclectic, elegant space is adorned with everything from floating vintage handbags and overblown chandeliers to the occasional stuffed beast. Guests choose from a two or three course epicurean prix fixe or opt for the tasting menu.

Factory Floor Dining

Wapping Food

16 Wapping Wall, between Monza St and Glamis Rd
+44 20 7680 2080
thewappingproject.com
🚇🚇 Shadwell
Open daily. Lunch Mon-Fri noon-3.30pm; Sat/Sun 1pm-4pm. Brunch Sat/Sun 10am-12.30pm. Dinner Mon-Fri 6.30pm-11pm; Sat 7pm-11pm.

Located in the grandiose industrial Wapping Hydraulic Power Station, Wapping Food is the culinary expression of the arts-focused Wapping Project. The cavernous space lends itself well to a dramatic brunch or dinner. Dishes have a distinctly English bent and include such mouthwatering classics as char grilled mackerel, venison pie and banana and treacle ice cream for desert.

Hotel, Restaurant & Bar

Viajante at the Town Hall Hotel

🔟7 Patriot Square, off Cambridge Heath Road
+44 20 7871 0461
viajante.co.uk
⊖ Bethnal Green
Open daily. Bar Mon-Thu 5pm-midnight, Fri-Sun noon-midnight. Restaurant: Lunch Fri-Sun noon-2pm; Dinner Mon-Sun 6pm-9.30pm. Set menu.

Located in a sumptuous former town hall-turned-hotel in this edgy part of town, Viajante's bar offers a gorgeous space to kick back with a cocktail. Designed by award-winning architects Rare, and complemented by local artists' and artisans' work, the space is thoroughly unique. Should you feel the urge to indulge in chef Nuno Mendes' full blown three, six or twelve course tasting menu, simply head to the restaurant across the imposing corridor.

A Festive Pint

Jaguar Shoes

🔟8 32-34 Kingsland Rd, at Drysdale St
+44 20 7729 5830
jaguarshoes.com
⊖ Old Street
Open daily noon-1am.

A most unique bar, Dream Bags Jaguar Shoes occupies two adjoining houses, which, in the 1980s, did indeed sell bags and shoes. The venue's current incarnation as a bar is a resounding hit. In an eclectic anything-goes atmosphere, enjoy the selection of beers on tap or a glass of wine with a stone-baked pizza from Due Sardi, freshly baked on premise. The intoxicating characters revelling on the Kingsland Road heighten the potency of your ale.

Clerkenwell & Islington
—From Workshop to Urban Loft

Wedged between Bloomsbury and Shoreditch, Clerkenwell was a centre of commerce and manufacturing before it developed into the vibrant urban community it is today. The area is home to some of London's more commercial designers and creative trades, which have turned many of its industrial buildings into lofts spaces.

In the 17th century, the area near the *Clerks' Well*, where London clergymen had performed mystery plays in the Middle Ages, became a fashionable place to live just outside the city gates. The settlement was a popular spa and resort when the Industrial Revolution turned the area turned into a hub for light manufacturing. Clerkenwell also developed a reputation as the print shop for the local left-wing intelligentsia—the Guardian was headquartered in the area until 2008.

Today, much activity is centred on Smithfield Market in the south and Exmouth Market further north along Farringdon Road. While the area around Smithfield Market—still a meat market today—has embraced a distinctly commercial character; pedestrianized Exmouth Market has a more bohemian feel. At the northern edges of the neighbourhood, King's Cross was synonymous with seediness until the Eurostar trains to Paris pulled into nearby St Pancras in 2007.

Islington, the mostly residential neighbourhood north of the Angel, was one of London's first suburbs. The area regained popularity as a place to live in the 1970s when its Georgian terraces where rediscovered by the middle class. Islington is also notorious as the spiritual home of Tony Blair's New Labour.

▲ ISLINGTON & KING'S CROSS (PAGE 66)

Swinton St
Acton St
Frederick St
Cubitt St
King's Cross Rd
Great Percy St
Lloyd St
Lloyd Sq
Wharton St
Lloyd Baker St
Inglebert St
Chadwell St
St John St
Arlington Way
Friend St
Hermit St
Amwell St
River St
Sadler's Wells 19

FINSBURY

Rawstorne St
Wynyatt St
Spencer St

Margery St
Yardley St
Wilmington
Merlin St   Hardwick St
Square
Pakenham St
Phoenix Pl
Calthorpe St
Farringdon Rd
Easton St
Rosebery Av
Gloucester Way
Myddelton St
Whiskin St
Wyclif St

Wren St
Caravan 7   Exmouth Market
15 16 Medcalf
Moro/Morito
Skinner St
Perciv

CLERKENWELL

Northampton Rd
Corporation Row
Woodbridge St
Agdon St

Gough St
Coley St
Rosebery Avenue
12 The Eagle
Bowling Green Lane
Clerkenwell Cl
Sekforde St
Hayward's Pl
Aylesbury St

Elm St
Mount Pleasant
Warner St
Baker's Row
Eyre St Hill
Ray St
Herbal Hill
Farringdon Lane
11 Three Kings

BLOOMSBURY (PAGE 11)
John St
Laystall St
Back Hill

2 The Zetter
Grea

Clerkenwell Rd

6 Work

Jockey's Fields
GRAY'S INN
GARDENS
Grays Inn Rd
Portpool Lane
Hatton Wall
Leather Lane
Saffron St
Turnmill St
Britton St
10 Jerusalem Tavern
Briset St
St John's Lane

St Cross St
Kirby St
Saffron Hill
Benjamin St Albion Pl
Eagle Ct
St John

Baldwin's Gardens
3 Prufrock Café
Hatton Gardens
Farringdon Rd
✚ Farringdon
Circle, Metropolitan, H'smith & Cit
Cowcross St
17 St

Brownlow St
Brooke St
Greville St

✚ Chancery Lane
Central
High Holborn
Furnival St
Shoe Lane
E Charterhouse St
W Poultry Av
Smithfield
Smithfield

N
200 metres

Nelson Pl
Remington St
Coombs St
H'stock St
Graham St
Wharf Rd
▲ ISLINGTON (PAGE 67)
Sturt St
Wenlock Rd
Taplow St
Bletchley St
Cropley St
City Rd
Pickard St
Murray Grove
Provost St
Micawber St
Hall St
Moreland St
Macclesfield Rd
Central St
Thoresby St
Windsor Ter
Wellesley Ter
Shepherdess Walk
City Rd
Nile St
King Sq
Dingley Rd
Hull St
Ironmonger Row
Dingley Pl
Mora St
Westland Pl
Britannia Walk
Vestry St
Goswell Rd
Lever St
Bath St
Cayton St
East Rd
▲ SHOREDITCH (PAGE 50)
Central St
Seward St
Norman St
Radnor St
Lizard St
Peerless St
Baldwin St
ST LUKES
Pear Tree St
Bastwick St
Mitchell St
Helmet Row
St Luke's Cl
Old St
Gee St
⊖ Old St
Northern
Look Mum No Hands ④
Whitecross St
Bunhill Row
Mallow St
Featherstone St
Leonard St
Old St
Garrett St
Banner St
Baltic St
Roscoe St
Golden Lane
Checker St
Dufferin St
Fortune St
Errol St
City Rd
Fann St
Tabernacle St
Brackley St
Sutton Way
Lamb's Passage
Bunhill Row
Worship St
Paul St
house Sq
⊖ Barbican
Circle, Metropolitan, H'smith & City
Beech St
Chiswell St
Silk St
Milton St
Finsbury St
Finsbury Sq
Aldersgate St
THE CITY
⑱ Barbican Centre

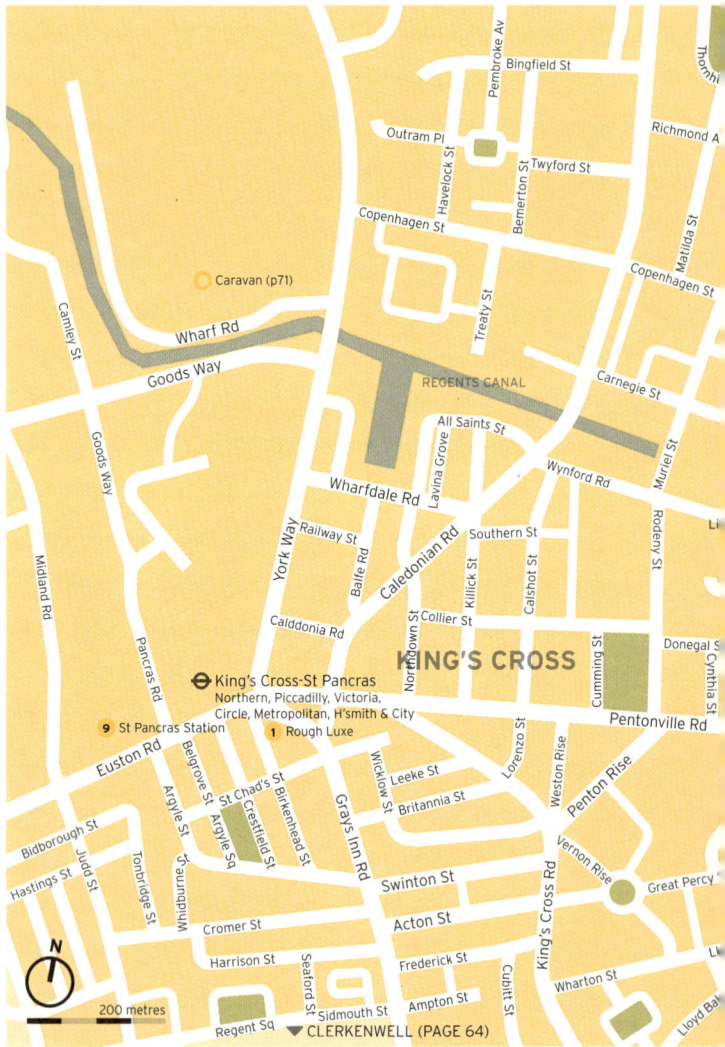

Bingfield St

Pembroke Av

Thornhi

Richmond A

Outram Pl

Havelock St

Bemerton St

Twyford St

Copenhagen St

Treaty St

Matilda St

Copenhagen St

Caravan (p71)

Camley St

Wharf Rd

Goods Way

REGENTS CANAL

Carnegie St

Muriel St

Goods Way

All Saints St

Lavina Grove

Wynford Rd

Wharfdale Rd

Rodeny St

Li

Midland Rd

York Way

Railway St

Balfe Rd

Caledonian Rd

Southern St

Killick St

Calshot St

Calddonia Rd

Northdown St

Collier St

KING'S CROSS

Cumming St

Donegal S

Pancras Rd

⊖ King's Cross-St Pancras
Northern, Piccadilly, Victoria,
Circle, Metropolitan, H'smith & City

Cynthia S

Pentonville Rd

9 St Pancras Station

1 Rough Luxe

Lorenzo St

Weston Rise

Penton Rise

Euston Rd

Belgrove St

Argyle St

St Chad's

Birkenhead St

Wicklow St

Leeke St

Britannia St

Vernon Rise

King's Cross Rd

Great Percy

Bidborough St

Crestfield St

Argyle Sq

Grays Inn Rd

Hastings St

Judd St

Whidbourne St

Tonbridge St

Swinton St

Cromer St

Acton St

Cubitt St

Wharton St

N

Harrison St

Seaford St

Frederick St

Ampton St

200 metres

Sidmouth St

Regent Sq

▼ CLERKENWELL (PAGE 64)

Lloyd Ba

Morland Mews

Barnsbury St

Barnsbury St

Richmond Grove

plevale Grove

Richmond Crescent

Thornhill Rd

Liverpool Rd

Richmond Av

Waterloo Ter

Napier T

B'shll St

Florence St

Sebbon St

Pleasant Pl

20 Almeida Theatre

Hawes St

Almeida St

Stonefield St

Milner Pl

Sh'gford St

Halton Rd

Cross St

Cloudesly Rd

Cloudesly Rd

Gibson Sq

Moon St

Studd St

Dagmar Ter

Popham St

Theberton St

Britannia Row

ISLINGTON

Barnsbury Rd

Liverpool Rd

Barford St

Gaskin St

Upper St

Essex Rd

Packington St

Queen's Head St

Cloudesly Pl

ISLINGTON GREEN

Elliott's Pl

St Peter's St

Cruden St

Raleigh

Chantry St

Batchelor St

Dewey Rd

Ritchie St

Bromfield St

Park field St

5 Kipferl

Devonia St

Rheidol Terrace

Tolpuddle St

The Elk in the Woods **14**

Charlton Pl

Gerrard Rd

Grantbridge St

13 Duke of Cambridge

hapel Market

Upper St

Duncan St

Noel Rd

Danbury St

Burgh St

St Peter's St

Frome St

ite Lion St

Baron St

Vincent Terrace

Claremont Sq

⊖ **Angel**
Northern

Colebrooke Row

Elia St

Quick St

Sudeley St

Rocliffe St

REGENTS CANAL

Myddelton

Chadwell St

St John St

Nelson Pl

Remington St

Coombs St

H'stock St

Graham St

Wharf Rd

ebert St

Square

Goswell Rd

Wakley St

City Rd

ver St

Sadler's Wells **19**

Arlington Way

Rosebery Av

Friend St

Paget St

Hermit St

Hall St

Pickard St

FINSBURY

▼ CLERKENWELL (PAGE 65)

King's Cross Glamour

Rough Luxe

❶ 1 Birkenhead St, at Euston Rd
+44 20 7837 5338
roughluxe.co.uk
🚇🚇🚇🚇🚇🚇 King's Cross St
Pancras
Doubles from £209 incl. tax
(Doubles without en-suite from £159
incl. tax); breakfast included.

Rough Luxe merges the luxurious
with the rough, creating a uniquely
urban hotel environment. The
patina of its distressed walls
melds seamlessly into such small
pleasures as sumptuous bed linen
and a special bottle of wine. The
decor is warm, hospitable and
inviting. A full spread is on offer
every morning for breakfast, which
can also be enjoyed outside in the
bijou courtyard. Cool and shabby
chic, the hotel goes beautifully
with its up and coming King's Cross
surroundings.

Converted Warehouse Hotel

The Zetter

❷ 86-88 Clerkenwell Rd, between
Aylesbury St and St John St
+44 20 7324 4444
thezetter.com
🚇🚇🚇 Farringdon
Doubles from £222 incl. tax; excl.
breakfast, available in-house.

Housed in a former Victorian
warehouse on St John's Square, the
Zetter is a sprightly, modern hotel
in an attractive historic setting.
The lobby bar offers staggering
views of the hotel's interior spiral
architecture and the on-site Bistrot
Bruno Loubet serves meals round
the clock. Rooms are similarly
pleasant and airy. Halfway between
Shoreditch and the West End
and close to all of Clerkenwell's
attractions, The Zetter's location
can't be beat.

Coffee Highlight

Prufrock Café

3 23-25 Leather Lane, between Baldwin's Gardens and Brooke St
+44 20 7404 3597
prufrockcoffee.com
⊖ Chancery Lane,
⊖ ⊖ ⊖ Farringdon
Mon-Fri 8am-6pm; Sat 10am-4.30pm; Sun 11am-4pm.

For a dose of absolutely stunning coffee in an urban market setting, head straight to Prufrock. In the midst of Leather Lane's mishmash of weekday market stalls and adjacent to the Hatton Gardens Diamond District, this spacious, comfortable café adds a dose of the cutting edge to an otherwise under the radar milieu. For those travelling further East, Prufrock also has a Shoreditch High Street location inside menswear boutique Present.

Coffee & Cyclist Heaven

Look Mum No Hands

4 49 Old St, between Goswell Rd and Central St
+44 20 7253 1025
lookmumnohands.com
⊖ ⊖ ⊖ Barbican
Open daily. Mon-Fri 7.30am-10pm; Sat 9am-10pm; Sun 10am-10pm.

Part bike repair shop, part café, Look Mum No Hands occupies a joyfully unpretentious space on Old Street, filled with colourful cycling paraphernalia, coffee cups and an assortment of local cakes. Its unique setup makes it the perfect stop over for a full English with a cup of tea or a local beer while exploring the city by "Boris Bike", taking advantage of Mayor Boris Johnson's popular citywide bike hiring scheme.

Austrian Café
Kipferl

5 20 Camden Passage, between Charlton Place and Islington Green
+44 20 7704 1555
kipferl.co.uk
⊖ Angel
Closed Mon. Tue 9am-6pm; Wed-Sat 9am-10pm; Sun 10am-6pm.

An Austrian café and kitchen on Islington's antique packed Camden Passage, Kipferl serves up a range of traditional Austrian dishes and cakes to go along with excellent coffees. The front café is a serene and sophisticated spot to partake in some people watching with your coffee and morning paper, or an afternoon slice of *Sachertorte*. The rear section is devoted to full-blown Austrian dishes, accompanied by wines and beers.

Aussie Roaster & Café
Workshop Coffee

6 27 Clerkenwell Rd, between St John St and St John's Lane
+44 20 7253 5754
workshopcoffee.com
⊖⊖⊖ Farringdon
Open daily 7am-6pm.

Originally the London offshoot of venerable Melbourne based roaster and café St Ali, Workshop Coffee has spun itself off into an independent bastion of the coffee bean. The Clerkenwell location incorporates an in-house roaster, insuring absolute freshness in every cup. All major meals are also on offer, including an award winning vegetarian breakfast. Service is laid back and the décor is mellow and inviting. When in Marylebone, stop by Workshop's second, café-only branch.

Exmouth Market Delight

Caravan

7 11-13 Exmouth Market, at Easton St
+44 20 7833 8115
caravanonexmouth.co.uk
◉◉◉ Farringdon
Open daily. Breakfast Mon-Fri 8am-
11.30am. Brunch Sat/Sun 10am-4pm.
All day menu Mon-Fri noon-10.30pm;
Sat noon-10.30pm.

A cheerful Australian establishment
at the Western tip of Exmouth
Market, Caravan serves a
spectacular brunch, a smashing
flat white and a gorgeous lamb
shank. Round the clock, this is the
place to go if you are craving some
of the modern-casual luster of the
antipodes. For the icing on the
cake, Caravan doubles as a coffee
roaster, guaranteeing premium
java to refuel even the weariest
of patrons. The café will open a
second location in King's Cross in
the summer of 2012.

Comfort Food

J+A Café

8 4 Sutton Lane, between St John
St and Berry St
+44 20 7490 2992
jandacafe.com
◉◉◉ Barbican
Closed Sun. Mon-Fri 8am-5.45pm;
Sat 9am-5pm.

Ensconced on the ground floor of
an old diamond-cutting factory,
J+A Café exudes a sense of cosy
wellbeing. Breakfast, brunch and
afternoon tea reflect a locally
sourced selection ranging from
freshly baked soda bread with
lemon curd to roast peppered trout.
J+A is the definitive place to go for
a healthy dose of comfort food in a
convivial setting.

Two Hours from Paris

St Pancras Station

9 Euston Rd, at Pancras Rd
+44 20 7843 7688
stpancras.com
🚇🚇🚇🚇🚇 King's Cross St
Pancras
Open 24 hours. Hourly departures to
Paris, Brussels and the Midlands.

St Pancras Station, celebrated for its
stunning Victorian architecture, is
the destination for Channel tunnel
rail services to Paris and beyond.
Erected in the mid-19th century as
a terminus for the main line to the
East Midlands and Yorkshire, the
structure only narrowly escaped
destruction in the 1960s. The
extensive renovations of the early
2000s added a distinct commercial
dimension, but its cosmopolitan
atmosphere and "Europe's longest
champagne bar" make it well worth
a visit.

Ancient Tavern

Jerusalem Tavern

10 55 Britton St, between
Clerkenwell Rd and Briset St
+44 20 7490 4281
stpetersbrewery.co.uk
🚇🚇🚇 Farringdon
Closed Sat/Sun. Mon-Fri 11am-11pm.

The Jerusalem Tavern has moved
around the Farringdon area since
the 14th century. It has occupied
its present, slightly slanted and
eminently charming incarnation
since 1720. Now owned by Suffolk
based St Peter's Brewery, the tavern
serves meals in addition to the full
range of St Peter's beers and ales.
A timeless spot to settle in with
a newspaper and a fresh pint of
ale while contemporary London
whizzes by.

Neighbourhood Pub

Three Kings

11 7 Clerkenwell Close, between Bowling Green Lane and Aylesbury St
+44 20 7253 0483
⊖⊖⊖ Farringdon
Closed Sun. Mon-Fri noon-11pm; Sat 5.30pm-11pm.

Set on the curvy climb of Clerkenwell Close in Farringdon, Three Kings is immediately noticeable for its festively colored red, yellow and green exterior. Step inside this welcoming pub and order a fresh draught beer before plopping onto a comfy sofa and soaking in some of the whimsical decor, including the head of a *faux*-rhino. The jukebox on the second floor is a draw for those in search of custom entertainment.

Gastropub Pioneer

The Eagle

12 159 Farringdon Rd, at Baker's Row
+44 20 7837 1353
⊖⊖⊖ Farringdon
Open daily. Mon-Sat noon-11.30pm; Sun noon-5pm. Lunch Mon-Fri 12.30pm-3pm; Sat/Sat 12.30pm-3.30pm. Dinner Mon-Sat 6.30pm-10.30pm.

A pioneer of the gastropub movement, The Eagle is still going strong after twenty years in the business. The menu has an Iberian bent and is unequivocally top notch. Specials are chalked up on a board daily, accompanied by good range of wines and beers. The gastropub's everlasting popularity with a diverse mix of bubbling personalities insures that there will always be a full house.

Duke of Cambridge

13 30 St Peter's St, at Danbury St
+44 20 7359 3066
dukeorganic.co.uk
⊖ Angel
Open daily. Mon-Sat noon-11pm;
Sun noon-10.30pm. Lunch Mon-Fri
12.30pm-3pm; Sat/Sun 12.30pm-
3.30pm. Dinner Mon-Sat 6.30pm-
10.30pm; Sun 6.30pm-10pm.

A delightful gastropub on a
charming Islington street, The
Duke of Cambridge was Britain's
first certified organic pub. Eighty
percent of produce comes from
the Home Counties and the
menu changes daily according to
availability of the freshest seasonal
produce. The selection of ales
includes two organic examples
produced in London itself, not to
mention a range of beers, ciders
and a wonderful wine list that spans
the globe but also includes some
exciting English bottles.

The Elk in the Woods

14 37-39 Camden Passage, between
Duncan St and Charlton St
+44 20 7226 3535
the-elk-in-the-woods.co.uk
⊖ Angel
Open daily. Mon-Fri 8.30am-11pm;
Sat 10.30am-11pm; Sun 10.30am-
10.30pm.

The Elk in the Woods is a unique
take on woodsy urban life,
complete with heads of wild game
and crackling fireplaces. The kitchen
serves all the brunch classics as well
as a hearty lunch and dinner menu,
with many ingredients sourced
locally. Head over for some New
Zealand lamb or rabbit and prawn
paella after a spate of antique
shopping on the Camden Passage.

Madrid Meets Morocco

Moro/Morito

15 34-36 Exmouth Market, between
Yardley St and Skinner St
+44 20 7833 8336
moro.co.uk
⊖⊖⊖ Farringdon
Open daily. Lunch Mon-Sat 12.30pm-
2.30pm; Sun noon-2.45pm. Dinner
Mon-Sat 7pm-10.30pm.

Award winning Moorish cuisine
created by husband and wife team
Sam and Sam Clark whizzes out of
the open kitchen and onto diner's
plates at this Exmouth Market
stalwart. The menu remains faithful
to pure North African and Spanish
recipes, rather than resorting to
fusion, and is highlighted by a
phenomenal mainly Spanish wine
list, including an excellent selection
of sherries. Guests can also drop by
sister restaurant Morito next door
for casual tapas at any time of day.

British Food

Medcalf

16 40 Exmouth Market, between
Yardley St and Skinner St
+44 20 7833 3533
medcalfbar.co.uk
⊖⊖⊖ Farringdon
Open daily. Lunch Mon-Sat noon-
3pm; Sun noon-4pm. Dinner
Mon-Thu 6pm-11.45pm; Fri/Sat 6pm-
10.20pm.

Housed in the former Medcalf
butcher shop, this restaurant
in the thick of Exmouth Market
specializes in locally sourced, mostly
organic British cuisine. Following
in the footsteps of its former self,
renowned for the quality of its
Angus beef, pike, wild salmon and
game, today's Medcalf is one of the
best spots in capital to enjoy some
authentic modern English cuisine.
The decor is jovial, highlighted by
local artists' work on display.

British Food and Drink

St John

17 26 St John St, between Charterhouse St and Clerkenwell Rd
+44 20 3301 8069
stjohnrestaurant.com
⊖⊖⊖ Farringdon
Open daily. Lunch Mon-Fri noon-3pm; Sun 1pm-3.30pm. Dinner Mon-Sat 6pm-11pm.

Located in a former Georgian smokehouse, this East London institution is one of the city's premier venues for British cuisine, paired with a superlative wine list. The Smithfield location is cavernous and atmospheric, doubling as a purveyor of fresh bread, wine and cheese. The space's colourful history includes stints as a Chinese beer shop and the headquarters of the publication Marxism Today. Since the restaurant opened in 1994, it has served solely as a bastion of the British culinary arts. The Spitalfields location is equally appetizing.

Arts & Architectural Highlight

Barbican Centre

18 Silk St, between Beech St and Milton St
+44 20 7638 8891
barbican.org.uk
⊖⊖⊖⊖ Moorgate
Daily performances. Refer to website for program.

A world-class performing arts complex, the Barbican hosts numerous classical and contemporary music concerts, theatre performances, film screenings and art exhibitions. The Barbican Centre forms part of the eponymous Barbican Estate, an expansive brutalist residential estate built on the rubble of World War II. Both the London Symphony Orchestra and the BBC Symphony Orchestra are based in the centre's Barbican Hall.

Premier Dance Venue

Sadler's Wells

19 Rosebery Av, at Arlington Way
+44 844 412 4300
sadlerswells.com
⊖ Angel
Daily performances. Refer to website for program.

The UK's leading venue dedicated to international dance, Sadler's Wells hosts an impressive array of productions from across the globe. Recent shows include a collaborative project between the legendary Pet Shop Boys and maverick choreographer Javier de Frutos, in his radical new take on ballet, and contemporary Brazilian Grupo Corpo's Onqotô (pictured). Located within an easy walk from the culinary hub of Exmouth Market, an evening of dance can be readily combined with a fabulous meal.

Islington Theatre

Almeida Theatre

20 Almeida St, at Upper St
+44 20 7359 4404
almeida.co.uk
⊖ Angel, ⊖⊖⊖ Highbury & Islington
Daily performances. Refer to website for program.

A local theatre with a global reputation, the Almeida hosts a range of British and international productions on its Islington stage. Plays presented at the theatre are often new takes on modern classics. The bright Almeida Café, located around the corner from Upper Street, offers patrons newspapers and wifi and often rotates its menu to reflect the provenance of current theatrical productions.

South Bank

—Riverside Arts District

South Bank is largely defined by the narrow band of acclaimed entertainment and cultural establishments on the southern banks of the River Thames. Its cosmopolitan qualities have recently been picked up by the more organically evolved locales of Borough and Bermondsey to the east, and South Bank's "string of pearls" is developing into a vibrant riverside neighbourhood in its own right.

The Thames' southern shores had historically lagged London proper in urbanity and sophistication. Over the years, the marshes of the low-lying flood area made way to a patchwork of light industry and working class dwellings. The area saw significant change in the wake of the 1951 Festival of Britain, when the arrival of the Royal Festival Hall redefined its riverside as an arts and entertainment district and the name "South Bank" was formally adopted. The opening of the Tate Modern (p84) in a former power station in 2000 and the extension of the Riverside Walk have stretched the area further down the river, reaching as far as Tower Bridge in the east. South Bank today is a vibrant quarter of bars, theatres and galleries, interspersed with pricey riverside loft living.

Borough, located on the main traffic artery across the Thames into the City of London, is closely associated with its eponymous market. Borough Market, situated under a number of railway arches since the 19th century, is a wholesale and retail food market renowned for the variety of its offerings. Beyond London Bridge, Bermondsey Street has become a focal point of a refined local restaurant scene.

Victoria Embank

Temple
District, Circle

RIVER THAMES

Lancaster Pl

Savoy St

Waterloo Bridge

Upper Ground

Coin St

Duchy St

Broadwall

Hatfields

Rennie St

Paris Gardens

Stamford Rd

Aquinas St

Colombo S

Meymott St

Cornwall Rd

Theed St

Whittlesey St

11 Skylon Grill
13 South Bank Centre

Roupell St

Windmill Walk

Greet St

Joan St

Concert Hall Appr

Mepham St

Exton St

Brad St

Belvedere Rd

Sandell St

Wooton St

Cons St

9

London Eye

Waterloo
Bakerloo, Jubilee, Northern,
Waterloo & City

14 Young Vic

York Rd

The Cut

Mitre Rd

Short St

Boundary Row

Leake St

Station Approach
Spur Rd

Waterloo Rd

Webber St

Ufford St

Chaplin Close

Valentine Pl

Coral St

Gray St

Baron's Close

Webber Row

Scooter Caffè 1

Lower Marsh

Lambeth Palace Rd

Westminster Bridge Rd

Launcelot St

Frazier St

Murphy St

Bavlis Rd

Dodson St

Gerridge St

Upper Marsh

Carlisle Lane

Lambeth North
Bakerloo

Pearman St

Morley St

Westminster Bridge Rd

N

200 metres

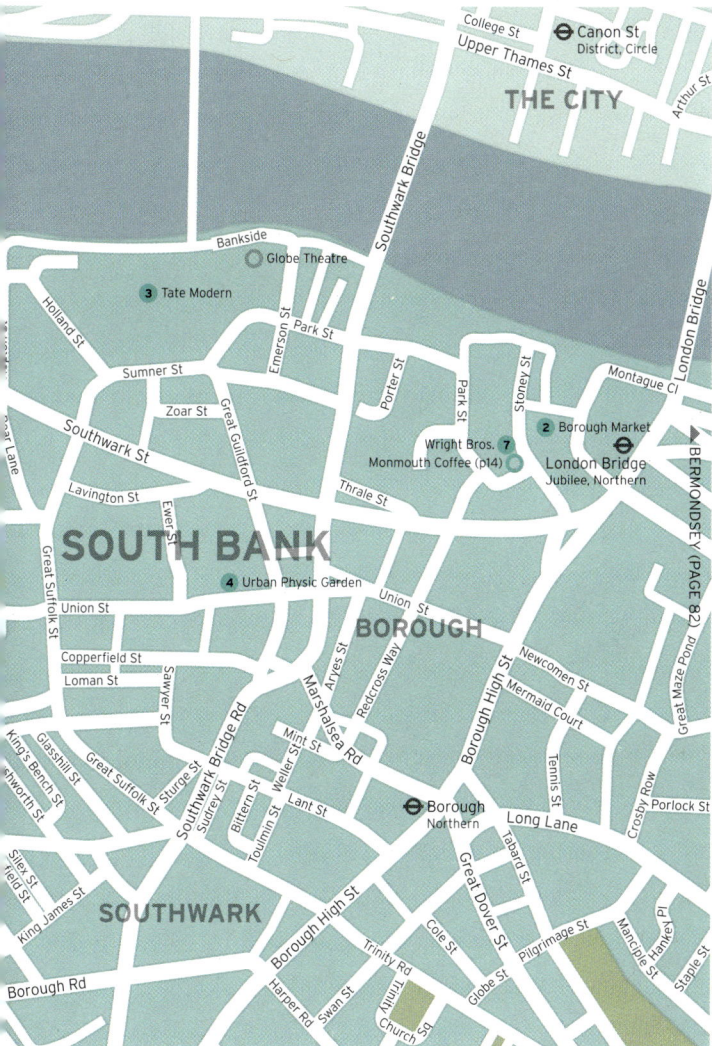

College St
Upper Thames St

Canon St
District, Circle

THE CITY

Arthur St

Southwark Bridge

Bankside
Globe Theatre

3 Tate Modern

London Bridge

Holland St

Sumner St

Emerson St
Park St

Porter St

Park St

Stoney St

Montague Cl

Zoar St

Southwark St

Great Guildford St

Wright Bros. 7
Monmouth Coffee (p14)

2 Borough Market

London Bridge
Jubilee, Northern

BERMONDSEY (PAGE 82)

Lavington St

Ewer St

Thrale St

SOUTH BANK

4 Urban Physic Garden

Great Maze Pond

Union St

BOROUGH

Great Suffolk St

Union St

Copperfield St

Loman St

Aryes St

Redcross Way

Newcomen St

Borough High St

Mermaid Court

Sawyer St

Tennis St

Crosby Row

Porlock St

Glasshill St

Great Suffolk St

Sturge St

Sudrey St

Mint St

Weller St

Lant St

King's Bench St

...worth St

Biltern St

Toulmin St

Lant St

Borough
Northern

Long Lane

Tabard St

Great Dover St

Mancple St

Staple St

Silex St
...field St

King James St

SOUTHWARK

Borough High St

Trinity Rd

Cole St

Pilgrimage St

Borough Rd

Harper Rd

Swan St

Trinity

Globe St

Church Sq

Tower of London

RIVER THAMES

London Bridge
Tooley St
Duke St Hill

London Bridge
Jubilee, Northern

St Thomas St

Joiner St

Hay's Ln

Battle Bridge Ln

City Hall

The Shard

Tooley St

Bermondsey St

Magdalen St

Holyrood St

Shand St

Weaver's Ln

Tower Bridge

Barnham St

Druid St

Queen Elizabeth St

Horselydown Ln

Great Maze Pond

Mellior St

Snowfields

Crucifix Lane

Druid St

Jamaica Rd

6 Delfina

BERMONDSEY

Crosby Row

Porlock St

Guy St

Weston St

Tyers Gate

White's Grounds

Kipling St

Leathermarket St

José 10   5 The Garrison

Tanner St

Tower Bridge Rd

Tanner St

Mantsey Pl

Long Lane

Morocco St

Lamb Walk

White Cube (p55)

Pope St

Maltby St

Maniple St

Staple St

12 Village East

Riley Rd

Pardoner St

Weston St

Wild's Rents

8 Zucca

Pizarro (p87)

Purbrook St

Law St

Decima St

Grange Walk

The Grange

Great Dover St

Rothsay St

Grange Rd

Prioress St

Alice St

Webb St

Page's Walk

Crimscott St

Tendall St

N

200 metres

Swan Mead

Leroy St

SOUTH BANK (PAGE 81)

Waterloo Café

Scooter Caffè

🔵 132 Lower Marsh, between
Launcelot St and Westminster
Bridge Rd
+44 20 7620 1421
⊖⊖⊖⊖ Waterloo
Open daily. Mon-Thu 8.30am-11pm;
Fri 8.30am-midnight; Sat 10am-
midnight; Sun 10am-11pm.

When New Zealander Craig
O'Dwyer opened his Scooter
shop on Lower Marsh Street, he
might not have expected that
the impromptu cups of espresso,
extracted from a sleek Faema
machine would become such
a draw. The coffee turned out
to be as much of a hit as the
scooters, and the now full-fledged
café is an eclectic and eccentric
neighbourhood classic with a
motory vibe.

Famous Produce Market

Borough Market

🟢 Stoney St, at Southwark St
+44 20 7407 1002
boroughmarket.org.uk
⊖⊖ London Bridge
Open Thu-Sat. Thu 11am-5pm; Fri
noon-6pm; Sat 8am-5pm.

London's most celebrated and
refined food market dates back
to the 13th century when traders
were obliged to move here from
crowded London Bridge. Borough
Market is famously located under
a number of railway overpasses,
and, since the mid-19th century,
beneath an extensive glass and
steel roof. A wholesale market to
this day, it is renowned for the
culinary variety of its retail offerings,
such as the Wine Pantry Tasting
Room, a purveyor of English wines,
and the Wright Bros. Oyster & Porter
House (p86).

Modern Art & Design
Tate Modern

3 Bankside, at Jubilee Walkway
+44 20 7887 8888
tate.org.uk/modern
Mansion House, Southwark
Open daily. Sun-Thu 10am-6pm; Fri/
Sat 10am-10pm. Free admission.

Housed in the gargantuan former
Bankside Power Station and sitting
squarely across the Thames form St
Paul's Cathedral, the Tate Modern's
setting lives up to its reputation as
one of Britain's foremost museums
of modern and contemporary art.
After contemplating a painting by
British icon David Hockney, why not
pop upstairs to the restaurant for
drinks and some dramatic London
views. For more traditional British
art, hop on the "Tate to Tate" boat
and head over to the Tate Britain
across the river.

Medicinal Herb Garden
Urban Physic Garden

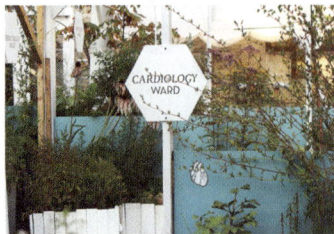

4 100 Union St, between Ewer St
and Great Guildford St
physicgarden.org.uk
Southwark, Borough
Closed Mon. Tue-Sun 11am-6pm;
June-August.

Located on a slice of neglected land
adjacent to a rail viaduct, the Urban
Physic Garden boasts a diverse
collection of medicinal plants and
herbs with healing properties.
Created by a group of designers
and volunteers, the garden provides
a platform for artists, gardeners and
health practitioners to explore the
role of plants in science, health and
the environment. Open during the
summer months, it also hosts talks,
workshops and film screenings.

Bermondsey Pub

The Garrison

⑤ 99-101 Bermondsey St, at White's Grounds
+44 20 7089 9355
thegarrison.co.uk
⊖⊖ London Bridge
Open daily. Mon-Thu 8am-11pm; Fri 8am-midnight; Sat 9am-midnight; Sun 9am-10.30pm.

A casually elegant gastropub replete with custom tattered furniture and French mirrors, The Garrison offers everything from brunch and dinner to the evening pint in a genial, bubbly setting. A hit with the local creative crowd, the gastropub keeps things inspired by changing its seasonal menu every eight weeks. The Garrison also hosts a weekly cinema night on Sundays.

South Bank Breakfast

Delfina

⑥ 50 Bermondsey St, between St Thomas St and Tyers Gate
+44 20 7357 0244
thedelfina.co.uk
⊖⊖ London Bridge
Closed Sat/Sun. Breakfast Mon-Fri 8am-11.30am. Lunch Mon-Fri noon-3pm; Dinner Fri 7pm-10pm.

Set in a converted chocolate factory, Delfina hosts a delightful gallery-like restaurant, adorned with modern paintings, navy blue chairs and white washed walls. A great place to grab an organic full English first thing in the morning or a casual but sophisticated lunch, Delfina is an ever popular brunch spot with the local artistic scene.

Borough Market Oyster House

Wright Brothers

🔅 11 Stoney St, Borough Market
+44 20 7403 9554
thewrightbrothers.co.uk
⊖⊖ London Bridge
Open daily. Mon-Fri noon-11pm; Sat
11am-11pm; Sun noon-9pm.

The Wright Brothers oyster and
porter bar is one of the highlights
of Borough Market. High stools spill
over wine barrel tables, and the
restaurant's effusive and uplifting
vibe is reinforced by the bubbles
wafting out of patron's champagne
flutes. The freshest seafood is
sustainably fished and delivered
daily from the shores of Cornwall—
Wright Brother's oysters come
directly from the restaurant's own
Dutchy Oyster Farm on the Helford
River.

Stylish Italian

Zucca

🔅 184 Bermondsey St, between
Lamb Walk and Long Lane
+44 20 7378 6809
zuccalondon.com
⊖⊖ London Bridge
Closed Mon. Lunch Tue-Fri 12.30pm-
3pm; Sat/Sun 12.30pm-3.30pm.
Dinner Tue-Sat 6pm-10pm.

Zucca offers scrumptious
modern Italian cuisine in a slick,
sophisticated setting. Located at
the southern end of Bermondsey
Street, the restaurant attracts a
buzzing mix of patrons and is very
much a part of the revived South
Bank scene. Squid nero with white
polenta, veal chop with spinach
and lemon and other *piati* are
accompanied by an extensive
Italian wine list.

Eastern European Restaurant & Bar

Baltic

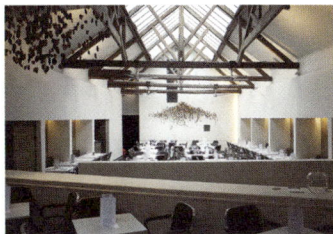

● 74 Blackfriars Rd, between Union St and Ufford St
+44 20 7928 1111
balticrestaurant.co.uk
● Southwark
Open daily. Lunch Mon-Fri noon-3pm; Sat/Sun noon-4.30pm. Dinner Mon-Fri 5.30pm-11.15pm; Sat/Sun 5.30pm-10.30pm.

Housed in an eighteenth century former coach builder's works, Baltic offers rustic Eastern European cuisine in an unusual and dramatic setting. A convivial front bar, serving blinis and dumplings along with the requisite vodka, gives way to a cavernous restaurant with a menu spanning the cuisines of Hungary, Georgia, Russia and Poland. The Pre-theatre menu is an excellent option for those planning on catching a performance at the neighbouring Young (p89) and Old Vic Theatres.

Sherry Bar

José

● 104 Bermondsey St, at Leathermarket St
+44 20 7403 4902
joserestaurant.co.uk
●● London Bridge
Open daily. Mon-Sat noon-10.30pm; Sun noon-5.30pm.

A cracking addition to the culinary hotbed of Bermondsey Street, José is a modern Spanish classic. Primarily a bustling sherry and tapas bar, the list of *jerez* is concocted by Masters of Wine associated with the neighbouring Wine and Spirit Education Trust, which ensures a rigorously curated selection. The tapas and deserts, including a highly recommended chocolate mousse, are equally stellar. For those seeking more substantial Spanish fare, owner José Pizarro recently opened Pizarro, an already wildly successful full-scale Spanish restaurant just down the street.

Thames River Views
Skylon Grill

11 Belvedere Rd, at Concert Hall Approach

+44 20 7654 7800

skylonrestaurant.co.uk

⊖⊖⊖⊖ Waterloo,
⊖⊖⊖⊖ Embankment

Open daily. Mon-Sat noon-11pm; Sun noon-10.30pm.

Perched on the top floor of the Royal Festival Hall, Skylon Grill is the relaxed yet sophisticated *à la carte* section of the more formal Skylon Restaurant. The aesthetic is retro-modernist 1950s and the views of the Thames and the West End cannot be beat. Cuisine is a sublime fusion of Finnish and French, reflected in the decor. The wine list is extensive and excellent. If you are just passing through pre or post-concert, Skylon's bar is a stunning place for a glass of champers.

Bermondsey Classic
Village East

12 171-173 Bermondsey St, between Tanner St and Long Lane

+44 20 7357 6082

villageeast.co.uk

⊖⊖ London Bridge

Open daily. Mon-Thu 9am-11.30pm; Fri 9am-1.30am; Sat 9am-1.30am; Sun 9am-11pm.

Exposed brick and comfy raw leather make this Bermondsey Street hit a cosy and refined choice at any point of the day or night. The restaurant offers a fusion of British and Continental cuisine, including such dishes as harissa tiger prawns, pan fried sea trout with Amalfi lemon and rabbit terrine. The wine list is exceptionally multicultural, offering an array of French, European, Australian and South African selections.

Performing Arts Centre

Southbank Centre

⑬ Belvedere Rd, at Concert Hall Approach
+44 20 7960 4200
southbankcentre.co.uk
⊖⊖⊖⊖ Waterloo,
⊖⊖⊖⊖ Embankment
Daily performances. Refer to website for program.

The Southbank Centre, London's largest arts complex, is centred on the Royal Festival Hall (pictured), the home to the London Philharmonic Orchestra. The modernist venue was built for the 1951 Festival of Britain, which aimed at showcasing the country's recovery from the War. The 1960s saw the addition of the Queen Elizabeth Hall, a second music venue, and the Hayward Gallery, a contemporary art gallery.

Sprightly Theatre and Bar

Young Vic

⑭ 66 The Cut, between Windmill Walk and Greet St
+44 20 7922 2922
youngvic.org
⊖ Southwark, ⊖⊖⊖⊖ Waterloo
Daily performances. Refer to website for program. The Cut: closed Sun. Mon-Fri 9am-11pm; Sat 10am-11pm.

The Young Vic hosts excellent and innovative theatre on its three stages. Although historically interconnected with the illustrious Old Vic theatre down the street, the Young Vic now operates as a fully independent venue. A 2004-06 refurbishment won the 2007 RIBA London Building of the Year award. The restaurant and upstairs bar, which spills over onto an outdoor deck overlooking The Cut, are ever filled with the buzz of theatrically charged conversation.

Hampstead & the North
—*Bohemian North London Village*

Hampstead, located in the hills of North London, has long held a reputation for the intellectual, liberal and artistic affinities of its residents. Separated from the bustle of London by Hampstead Heath, a hilly expanse of unrestrained parkland, Hampstead shares its laid back and bohemian feel with the nearby "villages" of Golders Green and Highgate.

A spa town since the 18th century, Hampstead saw more development when it was connected to the suburban rail network in the mid-19th century, and especially since 1907 when the newly opened Northern Line provided a fast link to central London. The town attracted a bohemian mix of writers, composers and intellectuals. By the 1920s and 1930s, it had become a hub for avant-garde artists and writers, many of them in exile from Soviet Russia and Nazi Germany. Despite its attraction to the wealthy, Hampstead has maintained much of its bohemian and liberal atmosphere to this day.

The Victorian enclave of Primrose Hill, a charming urban village on the northern fringes of Regent's Park, has a long history as a fashionable and exclusive place to live; the area is notable for its popularity with film and television actors. The adjacent hill, from which the neighbourhood derives its name, offers stunning views over central London.

Nearby Camden Town, although just a few streets away, could not be more different. Located at the junction of several rail lines and the Regent's Canal, its industrial legacy made way for its famous markets and an alternative music scene in the 1970s. More recently, the area has turned into a commercial tourism hotspot.

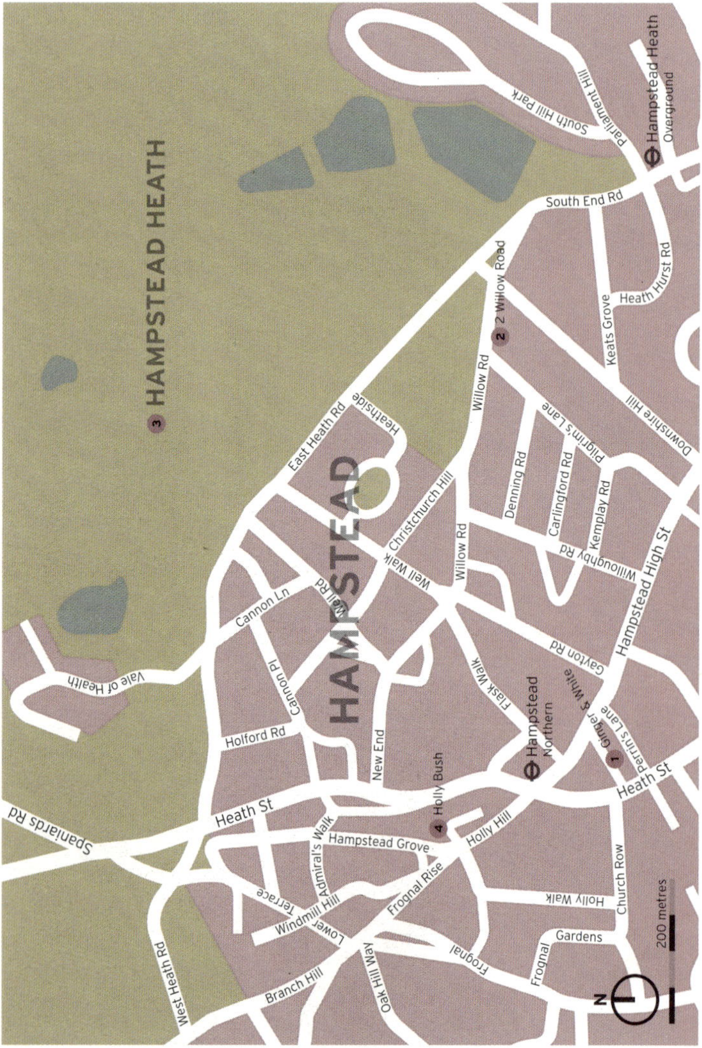

HAMPSTEAD HEATH

HAMPSTEAD

Hampstead Heath Overground

Hampstead Heath

South Hill Park
Parliament Hill
South End Rd
Willow Road
Heath Hurst Rd
Keats Grove
Willow Rd
Pilgrims Lane
Downshire Hill
Denning Rd
Carlingford Rd
Kemplay Rd
Willoughby Rd
East Heath Rd
Heathside
Christchurch Hill
Well Walk
Willow Rd
Hampstead High St
Gayton Rd
Cannon Ln
Cannon Pl
Flask Walk
Hampstead Northern
Oriel's White
Perrins Lane
Heath St
Holford Rd
New End
Holly Bush
Holly Hill
Church Row
Spaniards Rd
Vale of Health
Heath St
Admiral's Walk
Hampstead Grove
Holly Walk
Gardens
Lower Terrace
Windmill Hill
Frognal Rise
Frognal
West Heath Rd
Oak Hill Way
Branch Hill

200 metres

N

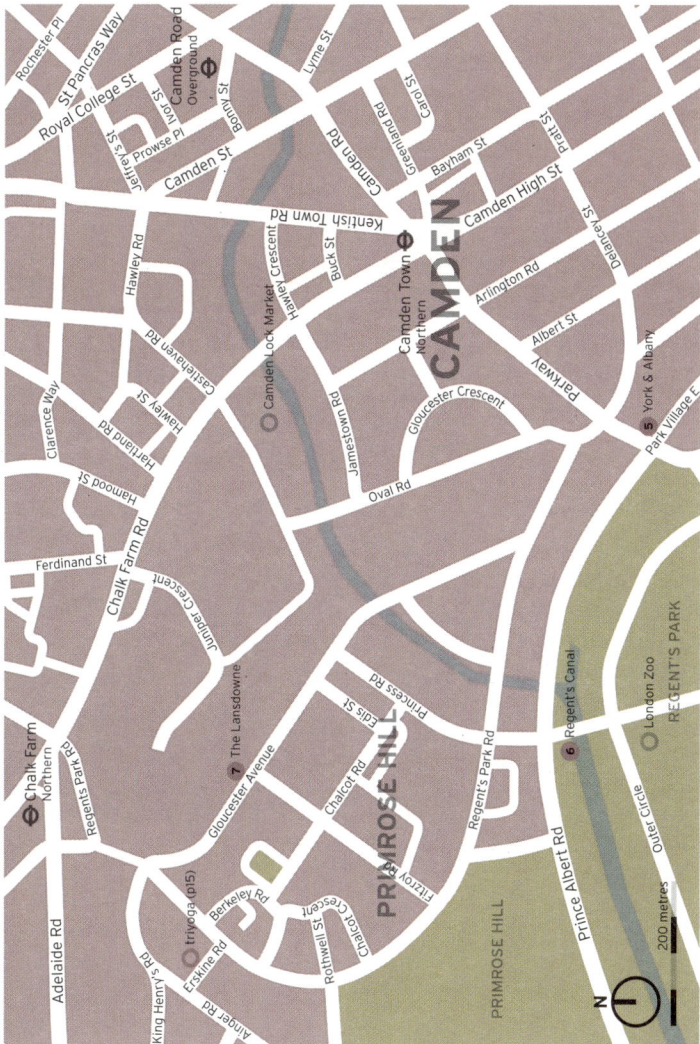

Rochester Pl

St Pancras Way

Royal College St

Camden Road
Overground

Camden Road

Jeffrey's St

Ivor St

Prowse Pl

Bonny St

Lyme St

Camden St

Greenland Rd

Carol St

Bayham St

Pratt St

Kentish Town Rd

Camden Rd

Camden High St

CAMDEN

Delancey St

Hawley Rd

Buck St

Hawley Crescent

Camden Town
Northern

Arlington Rd

Castlehaven Rd

Clarence Way

Hawley St

Hartland Rd

Camden Lock Market

Jamestown Rd

Gloucester Crescent

Albert St

Parkway

York & Albany

Park Village E

5

Hamood St

Ferdinand St

Chalk Farm Rd

Juniper Crescent

Oval Rd

REGENT'S PARK

Regent's Canal

Chalk Farm
Northern

Regents Park Rd

The Lansdowne

7

Gloucester Avenue

Edis St

Princess Rd

Chalcot Rd

Regent's Park Rd

London Zoo

6

Outer Circle

PRIMROSE HILL

Fitzroy Rd

Adelaide Rd

King Henry's Rd

triyoga (p15)

Erskine Rd

Berkeley Rd

Rothwell St

Chalcot Crescent

Ainger Rd

PRIMROSE HILL

Prince Albert Rd

200 metres

N

British Coffee Shop
Ginger & White

1 4a-5a Perrins Court, between
Heath St and Hampstead High St
+44 20 7431 9098
gingerandwhite.com
⊖ Hampstead
Open daily. Mon-Fri 7.30am-5.30pm;
Sat/Sun 8.30am-5.30pm.

Ginger & White is a top notch
"British Coffee Shop" located on
a pedestrianized side street in
the centre of Hampstead Village.
Influenced by the Continent,
Australia and New Zealand, the
café's owners are nevertheless
adamant about their passion for
British food, which they serve with
aplomb. Ginger & White purveys
some of the best coffee in North
London—and in a gorgeous
setting.

Modernist Home
2 Willow Road

2 2 Willow Road, between
Downshire Hill and Pilgrim's Lane
+44 20 7435 6166
nationaltrust.org.uk/2willowroad
⊖ Hampstead
Closed Mon/Tue. Wed-Sun 11am-
5pm. Mar-Oct. Admission £5.80.

Built in 1938, the modernist
residence at 2 Willow Road was
designed as a family home by
Hungarian-born architect Ernő
Goldfinger. As controversial as
it was avant-garde, the house's
construction was strongly opposed
by a number of local residents,
including novelist Ian Fleming, who
is said to have used Goldfinger
as inspiration for his James Bond
villain. 2 Willow Road has luckily
seen little change since the 1930s
and still contains Goldfinger's
innovative furniture and modern art
collection.

Heath & Woodland

Hampstead Heath

3 North of East Heath Road
+44 20 7332 3322
⊖ Hampstead
Public access.

A rambling expanse of heath and ancient woodland, Hampstead Heath lies immediately adjacent to the north and west of Hampstead Village. Long a popular place for leisure and repose for Londoners of all classes, the Heath came into public ownership in 1871 and was thus protected from further development at its edges. Parliament Hill in its southeast corner is one of the highest points in London and offers stunning views of the city's skyline.

Pub on the Hill

The Holly Bush

4 22 Holly Mount, off Holly Hill
+44 20 7435 2892
⊖ Hampstead
Open daily noon-11pm.

A glorious little gastropub dating from 1643, The Holly Bush is a jumbly maze of rooms perched high above the rest of Hampstead Village. The Sunday roast is a favourite, but lunch or a pint can be enjoyed here any day of the week. The fireplace and original features, including a creaking winding staircase, allow for some spectacular hop and malt fuelled time travel.

Regent's Park Hotel
York & Albany

⑤ 127-129 Parkway, at Park Village East
+44 20 7387 5700
gordonramsay.com/
yorkandalbanyhotel
⊖ Camden Town
Doubles from £186 incl. tax; excl. breakfast, available in-house.

Housed in an elegant 1827 Regency building designed by architect John Nash, the creator of neighbouring Regent's Park; York & Albany is chef Gordon Ramsay's first foray into the world of hotels. In addition to boasting a requisite on-site restaurant with views of the park, the hotel's decor is subtle, refined and warm. Its ten rooms have a decidedly British feel. In such an oasis of tranquillity, it is hard to believe that counter-culture Camden is but a few minutes away.

Walk by the Canal
Regent's Canal

⑥ Regent's Canal, between Primrose Hill and King's Cross
waterscape.com
⊖ Chalk Farm, ⊖ Camden Town
Public access.

Regent's Canal was built in the early 19th century to link north London to Britain's extensive network of canals and waterways. Commercial traffic declined with the rise of the railways and has since given way to leisure activities. The canal's towpaths allow for pleasant walks interspersed by clusters of moorings and the occasional canalside café. The section between Primrose Hill and King's Cross is a popular stretch, although intriguing corners also exist near Notting Hill and in the East End.

Primrose Hill Pub

The Lansdowne

7 90 Gloucester Av, at Fitzroy Rd
+44 20 7483 0409
thelansdownepub.co.uk
⊖ Chalk Farm
Open daily. Mon-Fri noon-11pm; Sat
10am-11pm; Sun 10am-10.30pm.

A charming gastropub in the thick
of Primrose Hill, The Lansdowne is
the perfect spot for an afternoon
pint or a delicious Mediterranean
inspired meal with wine to match.
In the colder months, settle at one
of the substantial wooden tables
by the crackling fire. If it's warm
outside, why not take in the bucolic
splendour of Primrose Hill while
sipping on a glass of rosé from
Provence at one of the outdoor
tables.

Essentials

Airport Transfer

The fastest way to travel into central London from any of its airports, except for relatively central City Airport, is by train. Taxis are a viable alternative and are readily available at Heathrow and City Airports. A commonly used car service is Addison Lee (addisonlee.com, +44 844 800 6677).

Heathrow (LHR): Heathrow Express train services (£18) connect the airport with Paddington station in central London in 15 minutes, every 15 minutes. A cheaper but slower alternative is the Underground's Piccadilly line (£5.30 at peak, 45 mins) with direct connections to stations throughout central London; trains depart every 5-10 minutes. There is no flat taxi fare to or from Heathrow; fares to the West End are typically £60 or more.

Gatwick (LGW): Gatwick Express train services (£17.90) connect Gatwick with Victoria station in central London in 30 minutes, every 15 minutes.

Stansted (STN): Stansted Express train services (£21) connect Stansted with Liverpool Street station in 45 minutes, every 15 minutes.

City Airport (LCY): The airport is directly connected to the Dockland's DLR light rail (£3.10 at peak). Taxi rides into the West End cost around £30.

Luton (LTN): Train services (£13) connect Luton Airport Parkway station with St Pancras station in around 30 minutes, every 10 minutes on weekdays. A short bus ride (£1.50) connects the local station to the airport.

Taxis

London's taxi drivers are famously familiar with the city's innumerable small streets and back alleys—in fact, drivers have to pass a test (the "Knowledge") which requires them to know the fastest route between any two streets or points of interest throughout the whole of London.

Quality does come at its price, and fares are in line with those of other expensive northern European capitals. A ride from Notting Hill or Shoreditch into the West End will cost £15 or more and takes around 20 minutes, if

London's notoriously congested streets permit. During rush hour and on weekends, journeys into central London can take significantly longer and the Tube or walking can be a quicker way to get around.

Although some taxis accept credit cards, drivers prefer to receive fares in cash, and payment by credit card is often discouraged through service charges.

Public Transport

The London Underground, also known as the "Tube" given its small diameter, is the oldest underground railway in the world and still provides one of the quickest ways to travel into and within central London.

The Tube operates from around 5.30am until between midnight and 1am, depending on the line, station and day of the week. Trains run fairly frequently, although lines have varying reputations: the Central, Jubilee and Piccadilly lines are reliable and usually run at short intervals, while services on the Circle, District and Hammersmith & City lines can be patchy.

There are six main fare zones. The areas covered in this book are exclusively in Zones 1 and 2. Heathrow Airport is located in Zone 6; City Airport in Zone 3. Ticket prices start at £2 for single journeys within Zone 1. Tickets purchased without using an "Oyster" smartcard, available at all stations and at many newsagents, cost as much as double. "Travelcards" for unlimited travel are available on a daily (£8.40 for Zones 1 and 2), weekly (£29.20) or monthly (£112.20) basis. See p104 for the Tube map.

Tipping

England's tipping culture is fairly reserved—tips are appreciated but not usually expected. Most restaurants add an "optional" 12.5% service charge to the bill which should be honoured in all but exceptional circumstances.

Safety

Although London, like any major city, has its rough patches, its central parts are generally safe. Note that in most areas there is little activity on smaller streets after dark, which makes these more prone to incidents should they occur. Neighbourhoods south and east of central London have historically been less prosperous and safe than those to the north and west.

Index

V

W

Y

Archway
Upper Holloway
Wembley Park
Hampstead
Tufnell Park
Neasden
Dollis Hill
Gospel Oak
Kentish Town
Willesden Green
Kilburn
West Hampstead
Finchley Road & Frognal
Hampstead Heath
Kentish Town West
Camden Road
Belsize Park
embley
Finchley Road
Camden Road
mbley Central
Brondesbury Park
Brondesbury
Chalk Farm
Camden Tow
Stonebridge Park
Kensal Rise
South Hampstead
Swiss Cottage
Mo Cre
Harlesden
Kilburn High Road
St. John's Wood
Kensal Green
Queen's Park
Euston
Willesden Junction
Kilburn Park
Great Portland Street
Maida Vale
Marylebone
Warwick Avenue
Edgware Road
War
Royal Oak
Westbourne Park
Baker Street
Regent's Park
orth cton
East Acton
Ladbroke Grove
Edgware Road
Oxf Ci
White City
Latimer Road
Notting Hill Gate
Paddington
Bayswater
Bond Street
Wood Lane
Lancaster Gate
Marble Arch
Green Park
Pi
Shepherd's Bush Market
Shepherd's Bush
Holland Park
Queensway
Hyde Park Corner
Stamford Brook
Goldhawk Road
High Street Kensington
Knightsbridge
W
Ravenscourt Park
Kensington (Olympia)
Victoria
m
Hammersmith
West Kensington
Earl's Court
Gloucester Road
South Kensington
Sloane Square
Barons Court
West Brompton

Bakerloo		Jubilee	
Central		London Overground	
Circle		Metropolitan	
Croydon Tram Link†		Northern	
District		Piccadilly	
Docklands Light Railway		Victoria	
Hammersmith and City		Waterloo and City	
Heathrow Express†			

○ Interchange stations
◉ Interchange with network rail services

† Croydon Tram Link, Heathrow Express and Watford Junction Station
are subject to special fare rates outside of the zone system
* London Overground Surrey Quays to Clapham Junction opens 2012

Clapham
Clapham Common

Leyton
Midland Road

Leyto

Leyton

rsenal
d

Stratford
International

Highbury
& Islington

Canonbury

Dalston
Kingsland

Hackney Central

Homerton

Hackney Wick

Stratford

Strat
High

ian
d
ry

Dalston
Junction

Haggerston

Angel

Pudding
Mill Lane

Hoxton

Old Street

Shoreditch
High Street

Bethnal
Green

Bow Church

Farringdon

Bromley-
By-Bow

Barbican

Mile End

Bow Road

Devons Road

hancery
Lane

Moorgate

Liverpool
Street

Stepney
Green

Langdon Park

St. Paul's

All Saints

Star

Whitechapel

lborn

Bank

Aldgate

Aldgate
East

Shadwell

Westferry

Poplar

East India

mple

Blackfriars

Tower Hill

Limehouse

Blackwall

Mansion
House

Cannon
Street

Monument

Tower
Gateway

Wapping

West India Quay

Canary Wharf

London
Bridge

Heron Quays

Southwark

Rotherhithe

South Quay

Waterloo

Lambeth
North

Borough

Bermondsey

Canada Water

Crossharbour

Elephant
& Castle

Mudchute

Surrey Quays

Island
Gardens

Kennington

Cutty Sark

Oval

Queens Road
Peckham*

Greenwich

Deptford Bridge

Stockwell

Peckham Rye*

New Cross
Gate

New
Cross

Elverson Road

Denmark Hill*

Lewisham

Brixton

Brockley

Credits

Published by Analogue Media, LLC
244 5th Avenue, Suite 2446, New York, NY 10001, United States

Edited by Alana Stone
Layout & Production by Stefan Horn

For more information about the Analogue Guides series, or to find out about availability and purchase information, please visit analogueguides.com

First Edition 2012
ISBN: 978-0-9838585-1-5

Every effort has been made to ensure the accuracy of the information in this publication. However, some details are subject to change. The publisher cannot accept responsibility for any loss, injury, inconvenience, or other consequences arising from the use of this book.

Printed in Spain

Printed on environmentally friendly paper made from 100% recycled material by mills that are FSC® certified.

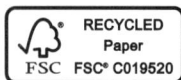

RECYCLED
Paper
FSC FSC® C019520

Analogue Media would like to thank all contributing venues, designers, manufacturers, agencies and photographers for their kind permission to reproduce their work in this book.

Cover design by Dustin Wallace
Proofread by John Leisure
Tubemap courtesy of www.london-tubemap.com © Mark Noad

Photography credits: all images credited to the listed venues unless stated otherwise. (9) Stefan Horn (12) left Soho House (13) right Robin Mellor (14) left Robin Mellor, right Monmouth Coffee Company (15) right Robin Mellor (16) right Jeff Knowles (17) both Robin Mellor (18) left Danny Elwes (20) left Robin Mellor, right Robert Turner (25) Stefan Horn (28) left James Volla, right David Loftus (29) left Prudence Cuming Associates Limited © Royal Academy of Arts, right Robin Mellor (31) right Kris Juhee Park (32) left MARC, right Jonathan Gregson (35) Stefan Horn (38) right Vencislav Nikolov (39) both Robin Mellor (40) left Neil Williams, right Robin Mellor (41) left Christian Smith, right William Meppem (42) left Soho House (43) Robin Mellor (49) Alana Stone (53) left Soho House, right Sarah Willcox (54) left Richard Bryant, right Chris Ridley (55) left Marc Quinn © Roger Wooldridge, right Alana Stone (56) left Andrew Moran, right Alana Stone (57) left Prescott & Conran Ltd (58) left Robin Mellor (59) right Steven Joyce (60) right Angus Boulton (61) right Jeff Metal courtesy of JaguarShoes Collective (65) Stefan Horn (70) left Marcus Peel (71) left David Robson, right vespamore photography - www.vespamore.com (72) left Johnny Pakington, right Long Black Ltd (73) left Arch MacDonnell, right Robin Mellor (74) left Robin Mellor, right St Peter's Brewery (75) both Robin Mellor (76) left Tricia de Courcy Ling (77) left Robin Mellor, right Justin Unsworth (78) left Laurie Fletcher (79) left Jose Luiz Pederneiras, right Burrell Foley Fischer LLP (81) Alana Stone (85) both Robin Mellor (86) left Robin Mellor, right Stefan Horn (89) left Jan Woroniecki, right John Carey (90) left D&D London, right Paul Winch-Furness (91) left Morley von Sternberg, right Ellie Kurtz (93) Stefan Horn (96) left Jonathon Gregson, right National Trust/David Watson (97) left Stefan Horn, right Robin Mellor (98) right Arne Bramsen (99) Gary Heasman.

About the Series

—A Modern Take on Simple Elegance

Analogue Guides is a series of curated city guidebooks featuring high quality, unique, low key venues—distilled through the lens of the neighbourhood. The guides seek to recapture specificity of place by highlighting aspects of the urban patina frequently lost under the corporate veil of large restaurant groups and ubiquitous chains.

Analogue is local: Analogue Guides delve into the very fabric of the city by taking the neighbourhood as point of reference. Each neighbourhood is complemented by a concise set of sophisticated listings, including restaurants, cafés, bars, hotels and serendipitous finds, all illustrated with photographs. The listings are supplemented by a set of custom designed, user-friendly maps to facilitate navigation of the cityscape.

Analogue is balance: The venues featured in the guides score high on a number of factors, including locally sourced food, tasteful design, a sophisticated and relaxed atmosphere and independent ownership. While we seek excellence across the board, we are not militant with regard to any of these elements but consistently pursue the greatest achievable balance when evaluating listings.

Analogue is convenience: Analogue Guides are designed to complement the internet during pre-travel preparation and smartphones for on-the-ground research. Premium photography and a select choice of venues provide an ideal starting point for pre-travel inspiration. At your destination, the guides serve as portable manuals with detailed neighbourhood maps and clear directions. You will instantly feel at home in the city.